ISBN 978-1-334-95342-2
PIBN 10783056

1 MONTH OF
FREE
READING

at

www.ForgottenBooks.com

By purchasing this book you are eligible for one month membership to ForgottenBooks.com, giving you unlimited access to our entire collection of over 1,000,000 titles via our web site and mobile apps.

To claim your free month visit:

www.forgottenbooks.com/free783056

English
Français
Deutsche
Italiano
Español
Português

www.forgottenbooks.com

Mythology Photography **Fiction**
Fishing Christianity **Art** Cooking
Essays Buddhism Freemasonry
Medicine **Biology** Music **Ancient
Egypt** Evolution Carpentry Physics
Dance Geology **Mathematics** Fitness
Shakespeare **Folklore** Yoga Marketing
Confidence Immortality Biographies
Poetry **Psychology** Witchcraft
Electronics Chemistry History **Law**
Accounting **Philosophy** Anthropology
Alchemy Drama Quantum Mechanics
Atheism Sexual Health **Ancient History**
Entrepreneurship Languages Sport
Paleontology Needlework Islam
Metaphysics Investment Archaeology
Parenting Statistics Criminology
Motivational

WHAT I REMEMBER
By MILLICENT GARRETT FAWCETT, J.P., LL.D.

" Let the community of the realm advise, and let it be known what the generality to whom their own laws are best known think on the matter."

SIMON DE MONTFORT in 1264

ILLUSTRATED

G. P. PUTNAM'S SONS
NEW YORK
1925

CONTENTS

ILLUSTRATIONS

WHAT I REMEMBER

Chapter I

THE ALDEBURGH OF LONG AGO

IT WAS MY GOOD FORTUNE to be born a member of a large family, and, moreover, in the younger half of it. I was either the seventh or the eighth child of my parents. I could never quite settle in my own mind which, for my eldest brother, born in November 1837, died in the following May, so his brief existence had come to an end nearly nine years before I was born in 1847 ; my only knowledge of him came from occasional references by my mother, who told us sometimes how, when her first little boy died, she had kneeled down and prayed God to take her too. I could, therefore, never really claim the special good fortune which is said to attend a seventh child ; but my sister Agnes and I were content to share this, and many other things, between us. Another piece of good fortune is that I have never known either poverty or riches, so that in my case the prayer of Agur was answered without my asking.

The year of my birth was the year of the Irish Famine and the repeal of the Corn Laws, and the following year saw the downfall of half the old autocratic Governments in Europe. Naturally, I cannot remember anything of these tremendous events ; but they may possibly have had an electrifying effect upon the whole atmosphere in which I found myself as a little child. At any rate, I began to hear about public events, and to think, in my childish way, about them at an early age ; for instance, I remember walking along the crag path at Aldeburgh (we always resisted with vehemence any Cockney attempt to call it The Esplanade, The Parade, or any such name) when I was young enough to be holding my father's hand and hearing him and listening with all my ears to his arguments, while he was persuading some of the leaders among the beachmen to volunteer for the Navy at the beginning of the Crimean War. I think this must have been in 1853 ; one man, I can recall perfectly, reiterating again and again that he was as ready as any man to sacrifice himself for his country, " But wolunteer, sir, I will not." I also remember very distinctly the death of the Emperor Nicholas in March 1854, and thinking in my heart that, of course, now the war would cease. I could not picture war except as a struggle between individuals, and if the man we were fighting with was dead, there could be no reason to fight any more. It was one of the strange things about grown-ups, I thought, that they never seemed to see the things that were so obvious to a child. The next thing I remember about the Crimean War is my father coming in at breakfast-time with a newspaper in his hand, looking gay and handsome, and calling out to all his little brood, " Heads up and shoulders down ; Sebastopol is taken." This was in September 1855.

There was a very cordial and friendly feeling between my father and the seafaring men at Aldeburgh. He was a merchant and owned a small fleet of trading vessels which plied between our little town and London, and also Newcastle and the North. Later he built vessels for himself at his principal place of business, Snape, a few miles higher up the river than Aldeburgh. He had some official position which connected him with the beachmen. I remember on his business writing-paper the, to me, mysterious words, "Agent for Lloyds and Receiver of Droits of Admiralty." The sound and look of the words *Droits of Admiralty* fascinated me. In the old days of sailing vessels the coast of Suffolk, and particularly the Aldeburgh bay, were very dangerous, and there was never a wreck without my father being present, and if there were lives to be saved he took an active part in the dangerous and difficult work. The rocket apparatus for sending a cord or rope over a distressed ship had not then been perfected, and lives were often lost in the vain attempt to reach and save mariners in ships which had been storm-driven on one of the shoals off Aldeburgh. The gun, three times fired, which summoned the lifeboat crew for active service was a familiar and none the less an intensely thrilling sound in our ears. Whenever the lifeboat was launched, even were it only for a practice, every man, woman, and child who heard the gun hurried to the beach, some to lend a hand, and all to see and wish and hope that the departing men would return in safety and bring their rescued comrades with them. It was a deep, angry sea where a tall man would be out of his depth three yards from the shore, and the great breakers in a storm beat with deadly weight upon men and ships alike. I remember one awful day, 2nd November 1855, when there were seventeen ships driven ashore or broken up on the shoals off Aldeburgh in my father's district. Everything that possibly could be done was done, but there was a terrible loss of life. My father received the official thanks of the Royal National Lifeboat Institution, engrossed on vellum, for his services on this occasion. This document, which now belongs to my nephew Philip Cowell, runs thus : *That the special*

*thanks of the Royal National Lifeboat Institution be pre-
sented to Newson Garrett, Esq., in testimony of his highly
meritorious conduct in assisting to rescue through the surf
nine out of the eleven of the crew of the Swedish brig "Vesta,"
which in a gale of wind was wrecked near Orford Low
Lighthouse on the 2nd November 1855.*

There was a family of seamen for which we ever
after felt a deep bond of gratitude and affection—the
Cables. My father and George Cable were taking a
leading part in making a human chain along a rope to
reach a shipwrecked crew in urgent distress and fetching
them off one by one. My father went first, Cable second,
and a good number following ; after doing this and
bringing in his man several times, my father showed
signs of exhaustion, and Cable said to him, " Look
here, governor, you have done this often enough,'" and
he took the leading place on the rope from my father
and assumed it himself ; he never came ashore again ;
the rope snapped between my father and Cable, as if
it had been pack thread, and Cable was washed away
and perished in sight of the gallant men who had undertaken the work of rescue. My father was again, and
by his own choice, in the place of the greatest risk,
which had just ended fatally before his eyes. We
were always taught by my mother to remember that
Cable had saved my father's life.

James Cable, the son of George just referred to,
was only a boy when all this happened, but as he grew
in years he developed into a very fine seaman, much
respected and well known all along the coast and in
the Lifeboat Society for combined courage and caution ;
for many years, indeed until old age compelled him to
withdraw, he was coxswain of the Aldeburgh lifeboat.
On one occasion this boat, under James Cable's command,
had more than usually distinguished itself, so that newspaper men from London came down to learn and retail

all the particulars of the brave work. They found Cable the very reverse of communicative; their only chance seemed to be to pump his narrative out of him in fragments, question by question. One of these, and Cable's reply to it, form a sort of epitome of his character.

Newspaper Reporter: "Now, Mr. Cable, you can tell me, I expect, how many lives you have saved at sea."

James Cable: "I don't know, I'm sure, sir; I don't keep no count on 'em."

This was the sort of thing that made everyone in Aldeburgh just love Cable, but he was not a bit spoiled—he was always the same simple, modest, upright man that his father had been before him.

Another incident of my childhood in connection with the lifeboat was an intense joy to me. The lifeboat gun had been fired, but only for a practice. The crew received three shillings a head for practice on a smooth day and five shillings on a rough day; this was a five-shilling day. We all ran off to the beach as usual, I, again, holding my father's hand. While the boat was still on the rollers one of her crew said to my father, "Come along with us, governor"; he replied, "I should like it, my lad, but you see I can't, I've got the child with me." Looking down on me, the sailor rejoined, "Little missie would like to come too, sir." There was no need for me to say anything. I was too enchanted at this unexpected adventure. The smallest cork jacket in the collection was found and slipped over my head, and we embarked. The seas broke over the boat as we crossed the shoal, and drenched my hair and shoulders; one of the kind sailors produced a pink cotton handkerchief from his pocket and said, "Here, missie, wrop this round your neck." Of course, I did so, and, of course, the pink handkerchief was soon as wet as the rest of my clothing. I was intensely happy, and never dreamed of being sea-sick.

My father was a very good sailor himself, and he never quite succeeded in ridding himself of the notion that to be sea-sick was affectation. One day, however, a little party of us, headed by my father and completed by a dog, embarked in a small boat for a sail. Before long the dog was sea-sick. My father was immensely astonished ; he said several times, " God bless my soul, look at that poor thing ; then it is *not* affectation, after all."

The Aldeburgh of my earliest recollections was very different from the Aldeburgh of to-day. It is true that its two ancient buildings, the church and the Moot Hall, still remain unchanged in essentials, but its ancient corporation has been re-formed. The two Bailiffs have been converted into one Mayor ; and the Council is elected by the vote of the ratepayers ; the dignified robes of office are retained, and so are the old silver maces dating from the reign of Queen Elizabeth, decorated by a large " E " with a crown.

Crabbe's house has entirely vanished, but in lieu of it a bust of our one poet has been put up in the church. He is still our one poet ; but a poet of to-day, Mr. John Freeman, has found our river, which runs parallel with the sea for about twelve miles before it is finally merged into it, a fitting subject for a parable in verse. A Turner engraving of Aldeburgh still exists, and is full of interest to those who wish to see how the old town looked to one who had the poet's vision.

At the time of my first visit to London, January 1858, the nearest railway station was at Ipswich, twenty-six miles away. I remember having felt in 1851, I being four years old, that the right thing had not been done by me in not taking me to see the famous exhibition of that year, but that I had been somewhat consoled for this slight by lovely bonnets of " drawn " blue velvet with pink baby ribbon and lace in the " caps " brought back from London for my sister Agnes and myself.

In 1858 the journey to London, the first I had ever taken, was one prolonged delight—first the drive of twenty-six miles in my father's carriage, himself, I think, driving, and then the railway train and all its wonders. I remember an old gentleman who travelled in our carriage and took a great deal of notice of us children, but whom we suspected of not being quite right in his mind, as he vehemently protested against the guard locking the carriage door, shouting out that he was a free-born Englishman and would not submit to being locked up.

The wonder of the London streets, especially at night, when the shop windows were not shuttered as they are now, but were brilliantly illuminated, made London seem to me a sort of fairyland. Our eldest sister, Louie, had married in the previous autumn ; we were her guests and were petted and made much of, to our hearts' content. One of our evenings was spent at Albert Smith's entertainment ; he was describing the journey of a party up the Rhine ; there were the senti-mental sister and the practical sister who lisped. The sentimental sister was reciting solemnly " Round about the prow she wrote ' The Lady of Shallot,' " and the practical sister comments, " I wonder what she wrote it with. Did she scratch it with a hair-pin ? " At this point, when everyone was laughing, a sort of managerial person came on the platform with a very solemn face and announced the attempt of Orsini to blow up the Emperor and Empress of the French on their way to the opera that very evening. This was my first experi-ence of anything approaching contact with the tragedy of revolutionary politics. This is also one of the points in my story to which I can affix an exact date : it was 14th January 1858.

But to return to Aldeburgh, as we did very soon after the unprecedented journey just recorded. Aldeburgh was a place very much without an aristocratic element in its population. It is true that there were three families, the Thellussons, the Rowleys, and the Wentworths, who belonged to the aristocracy ; but they lived quite aloof from the people of the town, and did not make the smallest impression on our lives. Mr. Wentworth, the Lord of the Manor, and Lady Harriet were hardly ever resident, except for a week or two in the partridge-shooting season. Mr. Rowley, with a large family, was, so to speak, hibernating in Aldeburgh, waiting to succeed to an estate and title then held by his unmarried elder brother in West Suffolk ; and the Thellussons were likewise lying low under the shadow of the great Thellusson lawsuit. I remember hearing Mrs. Thellusson tell my mother in an awed voice, " If we lose this lawsuit, dear Mrs. Garrett, we shall be beggars, absolutely beggars, on £600 a year." To me at ten years old £600 a year meant wealth beyond the dreams of avarice, and again I wondered at the strangeness of grown-up people. Old Peter Thellusson's extraordinary will and the portentous lawsuit to which it gave rise may have suggested to Dickens the great suit " Jarndyce v. Jarndyce," which forms the main theme of *Bleak House*.

Though not an aristocrat, there was a gentlewoman then living at Aldeburgh who had to the full the aristocratic instinct of service, of helping those less well off than herself to a fuller and better life. I think she belonged to what in the slang of the present day we should call the " New Poor." Mrs. James was the widow of a West Indian planter, one of those who had suffered financially from the emancipation of the slaves. She lived with great simplicity in a large house, and for all the years of my childhood she set apart a portion of this house to be used as a public elementary school. It seems now almost incredible that so late as the 'fifties and well into the 'sixties of the last century no public provision was made for the housing of a school for the poorer classes in Aldeburgh, nor, as I suppose, in the greater number of small towns and villages throughout the country. Mrs. James had several sons ; one a clergyman, the Rev. Herbert James, became the father of distinguished sons ; one, Dr. Montagu James, is now Provost of Eton, and well known in the world of scholarship ; another son, Captain James, was in the Indian Navy ; and we keep up very friendly relations with his surviving daughter, often talking over our recollections of old Aldeburgh. She remembers quite well returning from India in the days when there was no Suez Canal, and passengers were taken across the isthmus on camels or in palanquins.

The main interest to us in our Aldeburgh neighbours did not centre in the small group of those I have called the aristocrats, but in the Barhams, Mary Reeder, Mr. Metcalf, Mr. Dowler, the Vicar, and Bob Wilson, the old sailor at the Look-out Station at the top of the steps.

Chapter II

THE BARHAMS AND OTHER OLD ALDEBURGH FRIENDS

THE BARHAMS were in my parents' service long before I was born. He was groom and gardener : he drove the carriage when my father didn't ; he looked after the pigs, killed them when the fatal moment came, turned them into bacon, and was the gentlest, kindest, dearest, and most modest man in the world. Whatever in the nature of outdoor things we wanted, our first idea was to go and ask Barham ; he would look down on us with his rosy apple-cheeked face and smiling eyes, and say, as he put down his spade, " You are more trouble to me than all my money," and then proceed to do what we wanted. Years later, when most of us were grown up, my father had the idea, a suitable artist being handy, of having portraits painted of all the men who had been more than twenty years in his service. Barham, who was the senior and the most well-beloved, objected very much, and when the artist proposed to depict him with a pot of azaleas in his hand, downright refused to permit it. " If it had been a rake or a hoo," he said, he wouldn't have minded so much ; so a rake it had to be. Barham was a devotedly religious man, and belonged to a small dissenting community which had no chapel in Aldeburgh ; they had, however, a meeting-place on Aldringham Common, about three miles away. Some expressed surprise at

18

this, and especially that Barham chose this distant place of worship, involving a six-mile walk on Sundays after all his hard physical work on weekdays. But he was out-and-out an outdoor man, and I believe that the walk, the main part of which was over a lovely common covered with gorse and heather, with the sea shining in the near distance, was to Barham a real sanctuary of his soul.

Mrs. Barham was no less remarkable ; a tall hand-some woman with waving hair growing low on her forehead like the Clytie in the British Museum. She had charge of my mother's dairy as long as her health permitted. She was a most interesting conversationalist. We never went to see her without bringing away with us something worth remembering. She had two sons and a daughter. The elder son took service in London with Mr. T. Valentine Smith, with whom my father had business relations. This Barham became a first-rate wheelwright, and afterwards was placed in a responsible position on Mr. T. V. Smith's estate in Scotland. One of Mrs. Barham's epigrams related to the positions of trust occupied by her husband and elder son, the one in Aldeburgh and the other at Thames Bank, London. She said : " The sailors, they tell me that the last thing they hear when they leave Aldeburgh is someone hollering for Barham, and the first thing they hear when they reach Thames Bank is someone hollering for Barham."

The younger son, John, was an apprentice in a general shop in Aldeburgh. This did not suit Mrs. Barham's ambitions for him, and he was sent to London. Mrs. Barham's account of it was this : " John is a good lad, but I know my John wants polish ; so I am sending him to a situation in the Whitechapel Road." This poor John, whether polished or unpolished, was certainly vaccinated, but he died of smallpox in London in one of the epidemics which swept through it in the early 'sixties. About her daughter, Mrs. Barham was reticent—but obviously very sad. She was thought to have married well : her husband was a tradesman with a good business, but he was a drunkard and often and often the poor daughter felt she must have left him if it had not been for the two children. However, for the sake of her boy and girl, she endured to the end, which came while the man was still young. The next time I called on Mrs. Barham after this, she said, " You hev heard, no doubt, m'm, that my daughter hev lost her dear husband." A slight pause, in which I intimated assent, and Mrs. Barham continued : " You wonder, I expect, at my calling of him ' dear ' ; but he *was* dear, he cost her a many tears and sighs." And then she went on : " There was a great change come over William Marker before he died ; sometimes he would ask my dear daughter to read a chapter or to sing him a hymn, and when I think of the pore dying thief I hev my strong hopes of William Marker. But you know, m'm, you should see how them millers come buzzing about round my dear daughter. ' Mrs. Marker,' says one of 'em, ' I am desirous of becoming the purchaser of your business.' ' And so you will, sir,' she say, ' if you're the highest bidder.' Another come and say, ' Mrs. Marker, you must remember you hev lost your pore husband.' ' I hev, sir,' she say, ' but I hev not lost myself.' "

Once in our young days my sister Agnes and I went to a ball[1] at Saxmundham, Barham driving us in our old-fashioned carriage. On our return journey, about 2 a.m., there had been a slight fall of snow, and on the place in the Aldeburgh road where it crosses the common there were no hedges to mark its course. The horses wandered from the road and

[1] At this ball, and at several others, we used to meet members of the Cavell family, before the birth of Edith Cavell, the heroic nurse who was shot by the Germans in Brussels about fifty years later, on 15th October 1915.

went up a fairly steep bank, with the result that
the carriage was overturned ; my sister and I, in our
satin slippers, found ourselves about two miles from
home with no choice but to walk the rest of the way.
Barham, of course, was on his feet even before we were
on ours, seeing to the horses, who stood perfectly still.
He remained guarding the carriage and its contents
until he obtained help, while we walked home. The
tragedy came next day. My father was furiously angry
with Barham—said he must have been drunk, which was
to us absurd. Everyone but Barham admitted that
he might have been a bit sleepy. But Barham wouldn't
even admit this, and my father dismissed him. Barham
went home very quietly ; he maintained that he was
not drunk and was not asleep, but that it was impossible
in that place under a slight fall of snow to see the road.
When Barham reappeared he was in his Sunday clothes ;
he did not take himself off in a temper, he merely said
that he wasn't going to leave ; he knew when he had
got a good master, and master ought to know when he
had got a good servant. Then my father fumed and
raged, and stuck to it that Barham should leave. Our
one hope was Mrs. Barham, and she did not fail us.
Her own account of it was that on the second morning
after the dismissal it was cold and wet, and she persuaded
Barham to have a cup of tea in bed. " Then I went
down and made him a nice cup of tea and a slice of hot
buttered toast, like I know he liked, and I set down
by his side till he had finished, and then I said to him,
gentle like, 'Now, Barham, you was asleep, wasn't
you ?' and Barham said he might ha' been." And
thus ended our domestic tragedy. Some months after,
James Smith, our eldest sister's husband, being in
Aldeburgh, Barham came in to his wife with a smile
on his face, and she asked him what he was smiling at.
Mrs. Barham must tell the rest. " ' Mr. Smith,' he

say, 'hev been a joking o' me about upsetting my young ladies.' 'Barham,' I say, '*I wonder at you, jokin' on that solemn occasion.*'"

I could really go on almost indefinitely reporting Mrs. Barham's conversation. She was not only a very good talker, but was clever all round in many kinds of work. She made most elaborate patchwork quilts of geometrical design, of her own devising ; and for us, her own young ladies, as she called us, she aimed at making them entirely of silk. When she was working at one of these quilts, made up by small octagons fitted together with minute nicety, my sister Alice (Mrs. Cowell) came in to see her and found that Mrs. Barham was running short of a pale cream-coloured silk, which was needed to finish one of the four corners of the design in a quilt to be presented either to Agnes or myself. " She see in a minute how I was sitivated and how short I was of that light ; well, she went home and sent me two bodies of frocks dirackly—soo like a sister." Each of the little octagons was tacked on to a paper of the exact shape required, and when the sewing together was accomplished the great work began of taking out all the paper framework on which the quilt had been built up. " I tell Barham," she would say, " that he mustn't expect no hot victuals when I am taking out the papers."

When quilts had been made for all the six daughters of my father's house, the daughters-in-law began to think (one of them, at any rate) that their turn was coming. But Mrs. Barham quickly nipped this expectation in the bud. " Noo, Mrs. Edmund," she replied to a rather pointed inquiry, " I shall niver make another ; my husband say I am not to, and," turning to me for confirmation, " we must always do what our husbands say, mustn't we, ma'am ? " I rejoined, " I wonder at you, Mrs. Barham, talking like that, when everybody knows that Barham does what you say a great deal more than you do what he says." A smile and a knowing look came into her face, and she rejoined, slyly, " Well, m'm, I du say that if our oon way is a good way there's nothing like hevin' it." (The " oth " in nothing should be pronounced like the " oth " in bother.) This became quite a familiar saying in our family.

When my husband became Postmaster-General in 1880 no one was more interested in his new official position than Mrs. Barham ; it appeared that she had a great-nephew in the Post Office whose abilities she thought were worthy of a better kind of work than that entrusted to him. She did not fail to raise the subject when I was next in her company. She had had her great-niece with her not long before, a sister of the young man in the G.P.O. " Yes, m'm, Jennie was here, and I thought I would talk to her about her brother. I didn't like to say to her straight out, ' What is your brother Willie's character ? ' but I worked up to it kind of gradual ; soo, when we was settin' at our teas I say to her, ' Jennie, dear girl, do your brother Willie drink ? ' " This gradual approach to the subject had very satisfactory immediate results, for Jennie was able to give her brother a clean bill of character, but unfortunately for her there were so many young fellows in the G.P.O. with similar qualifications that it did not lead to his immediate promotion.

Of a somewhat important funeral in Aldeburgh, Mrs. Barham was pleased to express her approval of the arrangements made. " The family all following, husbands and wives walking together. Now some people make the eldest son walk first, along with the eldest daughter, and the second son along with the second daughter, right down to the ind—and then the pore ' laws ' all alone by themselves." It was the first time any of us had heard sons- and daughters-in-law called

" the pore laws," and the expression took root. One of my nephews-in-law to this day always signs himself when writing to me " Your affectionate pore law." One more story of Mrs. Barham shall be my last. It has a pathetic note. Her dear daughter, Mrs. Marker, had died not long after the death of her husband, and the two children, a boy and a girl, the former about four years junior to the latter, were left without either father or mother. The girl in this position developed a motherly and protective feeling towards the boy. When they both had holidays at their respective schools she would seek him out and take him for some little excursion. On one of these excursions she took him to Beccles, where there is an attractive river and a nice woman who let out boats to hire by the hour ; the two children presented themselves at her house and said they wanted a boat. And now Mrs. Barham must finish the story : " The woman, she looked 'em up and down, and then she say, ' What could your father and mother be thinking of to let you two dear children come here all alone by y'rselves to goo out in a boat ? ' And then the two pore children bursted out crying, and said their father and mother was both dead : and the woman, oh ! she was so sorry you can't think : she couldn't do enough for 'em. She let 'em hev a boat without charging them nothin' for it, and when they came back she say to them, ' Now, you two dear children, you go down into my garden and gather anything you like that grows there.' But what was the good o' that ? They didn't want nothin' out of the woman's garden."

There was a remarkable old lady who had lived in Aldeburgh all her life, and remembered in minute detail the chief events of the Napoleonic Wars. Her name was Mary Reeder ; she was often given brevet rank and called Mrs. Reeder. In middle life she had been a nurse in the Rowley family, and had specially devoted herself to a delicate child. She lived to be nearly one hundred, and directed in her will that the church bells should ring a merry peal at her funeral in lieu of the usual solemn tolling. She lived in her own cottage, bequeathed to her by her father. It had a pleasant little garden in front and at the back. Mary objected to chance acquaintance and indiscriminate greetings, and would say, " If I goes out in my front, one and another passing says, ' Good day, Mrs. Reeder,' or ' Hope you are well, Mrs. Reeder.' I don't want none of that, so when I wants the air, I goes out in my back." Her father had been in the Navy, and he and four other Aldeburgh men had been taken prisoners by the French about 1798. " When none of the five came back, and nothing was heard of them by their wives, four on 'em thought their husbands was dead and put on black and widders' caps : but my mother, she say, ' Noo, I will niver put on black for Joo Reeder not till I *know* he's dead, not if I can afford it iver soo.' Soo she put me out to nurse and went into service again herself. Well, when five years after that they all came back,[1] alive and well, you should ha' seen how silly them other women looked as had made certain their husbands was dead. But my father, he bought this house, and my mother came back to live with him in it. Oh ! it *was* a wretched place then, the roof all to pieces, earth floor in the kitchen, and no comfort anywhere : and my mother, she say, ' Joo Reeder, Joo Reeder, this *is* a place to bring a woman to l ' But my father he was as merry as could be. Sailor-like, as soon as he had lighted a fire and put a kittle on to boil, he thought he'd got a home : and he worked away at it and got it all to rights in noo time." She used also to tell how on another occasion her father, having just been released on furlough from

[1] I think this must have been during the Peace of Amiens, when prisoners on each side were released.

his ship and put ashore at Portsmouth, was proceeding to *walk* to Aldeburgh, a distance, I suppose, of some 150 miles, when he was taken by the Press Gang and sent back into active service again. When I contrast this with the treatment of our men in the late war, I cannot help feeling that, whatever may be its faults, a democratic Government is more humane and more intelligent than the old autocracies.

When Mary Reeder was about seventy, and very hard pressed to make ends meet, for she had very little besides her cottage, my father arranged to give her a pension of so many shillings a week as long as she lived on condition that the cottage was to be his when she died. Well, she lived and lived and lived : and we were very glad she did : it was she who was disturbed by it. She used quite to worry us by harping on the subject every time we saw her. She constantly wanted to give my mother a pretty little set of silver spoons which she possessed, my mother as constantly declining them, saying she enjoyed very much more seeing them on Mary's table than she would if they were locked up in the plate chest at Alde House, but Mary had got the subject on her brain, and could not leave it alone. " I ha' lived out of the course of nature," she argued, " and I want to die an honest woman." My mother was equally determined, but Mary left her the spoons in her will. An honest woman she certainly was : some question arose as to her exact age : was she really one hundred or only ninety-eight or so ? " It is very easy to settle that," said my mother, " ask the Vicar to give you a copy of the entry of your birth in the parish register." Mary agreed, and my mother added, " The charge for that, you know, Mary, is 3s. 6d. " The reply came as quick as lightning, " And I have got it riddy for him, too." When in 1870 the municipal franchise was given to women ratepayers, Mary became a voter, and my father being keen on the return of a certain candidate, asked the daughters who were at home to canvass the women electors. When they came to Mary Reeder's house they found with her an old man named Taylor—Billy Taylor he was always called. My sisters did not canvass him, for he saved them the trouble by volunteering the following information : " When my pore dear sister lay a-dying, ' Willam,' she say to me, ' when there's any vooting' goin' forrard, du you always voot same as Mr. Newson Garrett, be that blew, yaller, or rad ' : and so I du." The point of this lay in my father lately having changed over from the Conservative to the Liberal side in politics. My father didn't like this story about Billy Taylor at all.

Other friends came to live in Aldeburgh in the 'sixties : Mr. and Mrs. Percy Metcalf. He came from the Tyne, and was a shipbuilder by profession : he built some ships at Snape for my father, and made great friends with Sawyer, the head carpenter, and Felgate, the shipwright, who were already in my father's service. But what made all the difference to the rest of our lives was his passion for music. It was he who introduced us to the great world of music—Bach, Mozart, and Handel. He was less enthusiastic about Beethoven ; and Wagner, I think, he had never heard of. Mozart was the god of his idolatry, and Spohr. I can hear now my sister Agnes singing Spohr's " Who calls the Hunter to the Wood ? " with the piano accompaniment in Mrs. Metcalf's rather inadequate hands, Mr. Metcalf playing the horn obligato, taking the horn from his lips from time to time to say to his wife quite good-naturedly, " What a fool you are, my dear." He opened a new world of music to us, and gave us a peren-nial spring of consolation, hope, and endurance which has never failed us. The local concerts at Aldeburgh became quite a different thing after the arrival of the

Metcalfs : he would sing songs out of *Figaro* and
Don Giovanni in a way that made the audience hardly
know whether they were standing on their head or their
heels : and even Mrs. James, usually so reserved,
would say it reminded her "of her naughty days,"
when she used to go to the opera. After one of his
Don Giovanni songs there was a great roar of applause,
and he flung himself back on his seat and exclaimed
sotto voce, " I thought the fools would like it."

In after-years my sister Agnes's friendship with
Sir Hubert and Lady Maud Parry gave us another
great musical friend, of whom I shall have more to tell
in a later chapter.

Chapter III

MY FATHER AND MOTHER

WHAT I HAVE WRITTEN already may, I hope, give some indication of my father's personality. I cannot pretend to write with any detachment either of him or of my mother. My father was a handsome man, of the straight-featured Scandinavian type. In appearance he was not unlike Garibaldi : but the portrait of Walt Whitman at the beginning of *Specimen Days* is so like him that it might have passed, even among his near relations, for a portrait of himself. I have tested this by showing it to nieces and nephews and, covering the name, have asked, " Who is this ? " They have answered at once, " Uncle Newson."

There is another portrait of Walt Whitman in his old age, now in the Metropolitan Museum of New York, and here reproduced, which is also extraordinarily like my father when he was old. It is so like him that I can never see it without a thrill. The eldest of my great-nieces, Lesley, now Mrs. More, daughter of Sir George and Lady Gibb, writes to me of what she remembers of her great-grandfather : " My memory of him is bound up with a vast expanse of white beard . . . and somewhere just above glowed two sapphires with a fire behind them."

We had been told by Mrs. Barham (an older contemporary of my father) that he was the most beautiful child she had ever seen ; fair-haired, of a bright complexion,

" ruddy and withal of a beautiful countenance and goodly to look upon," like David. He was a great contrast in this respect to his sister and two brothers, who were dark even to the point of swarthiness. His temperament was sanguine, generous, daring, impulsive, and impatient, and I am afraid I must add, quarrelsome. There were very few in our little circle at Aldeburgh with whom from time to time he did not quarrel desperately. He quarrelled badly with his elder brother, Richard, of Leiston. Sometimes he quarrelled so fiercely with our clergyman, Mr. Dowler, that going to church on Sunday became a positive scandal ; then we were all marched off to the little dissenting chapel in the High Street, and it entertained us very much to see with what deference we, even the little children of our party, were greeted by the usual habituées of the place. Once about the time of the birth of my dearest brother, Sam, the war between my father and the Vicarage waxed so hot that he swore that Mr. Dowler should not christen the new baby : Sam was therefore taken, suitably escorted, to be christened at Snape Church, a beautiful little fifteenth-century building with a font much more ancient.[1]

My father had built up a considerable malting business at Snape : it was conveniently situated on the Alde, so that malt and other things could be shipped thence : and when railways became a practical proposition in our part of Suffolk my father exerted himself successfully to get a branch line, for goods only, extended to Snape. The junction is between Wickham Market and Saxmundham, and it is one of my joys to this day to look out of the railway carriage window at this point and see the

[1] There is a tale hanging to this which I feel I must not leave out. Some thirty years later my brother was walking with his eldest boy in the neighbourhood of Snape Church, and, pointing to it, said, " Father was christened in that church, Douglas." Whereupon the child replied, " What a *menjously* old church it must be ! "

WALT WHITMAN.

(Metropolitan Museum of New York)

To face page 30

masts of ships rising up apparently out of the trees and meadows of rural Suffolk.

Snape Bridge is of importance strategically, as we found out during the war, for it is the main place where heavy-wheeled traffic can cross the Alde. One of my Leiston cousins saw it marked very prominently in a German map circulated among German officers in the late war.

For many years, from the 'fifties and 'sixties of the last century, our family migrated from Aldeburgh to Snape during the winter months. My father's main business was then at Snape. This was constantly growing, while his business in Aldeburgh, since the arrival of the railway, was as constantly diminishing. My father adapted himself with characteristic energy to the new situation. There was no house at Snape where we could live, so he at once built one, in the bungalow style : a one-storied house which could be extended at discretion. Its advantage from the business point of view was obvious, and, as its position shortened my father's driving journeys to nearly all the markets at which he bought barley, it considerably lessened the fatigue and wear and tear of his life. Malting can only be carried on in the cool months of the year : it generally stops in May and is resumed in October or November. For many years, therefore, Snape was our winter, and Aldeburgh our summer, home. Often and often I remember my father returning from his more distant markets, having driven himself in an open dog-cart, his hair and beard fringed with icicles. He was fond of horses, and rode himself almost daily until nearly the end of his life. He taught us all to ride, and mounted us on Shetland ponies as soon as we were old enough to sit on a saddle. It was a great pride to him to take out a cavalcade. He was a fearless driver, and it was quite an interesting adventure driving with him. " Would you like to see the new house that So-and-so is building over there?" he would say, pointing with his whip across the common. Of course we did like, and then we drove straight over the common where there was no road and where the vehicle was often very much out of the perpendicular. He met, naturally, with many accidents, but none of a serious kind : his horse would arrive home sometimes without the trap, and then a search party would set out, usually meeting my father before long, laughing at his misadventure.

It was one of our family jokes that he kept up this habit of upsetting himself even when age and infirmity had reduced him to a bathchair : it was a bathchair with a pony to draw it, and he even managed to upset himself in this, and was found laughing to himself, the pony standing close by perfectly quiet, my father still encased in his wrappings, chair and all, like a hermit crab in its shell.

My father, until he was past middle life, believed himself to be a Conservative, but he was not in the least a Conservative in temperament. Everything new appealed to him, rather as it did to the Athenians of old. He welcomed railways with both hands, though they destroyed his carrying trade at Aldeburgh. If he had lived in the twentieth century I am certain he would have welcomed motor-cars, aeroplanes, and wireless. About the early 'sixties it occurred to him that he was not a Conservative, and he wrote to Sir Fitzroy Kelly, then M.P. for East Suffolk, for whom he had hitherto voted, that he had changed his politics and should thenceforth support the Liberal Party. His delight in novelties showed itself in various ways. I forget the exact date when Turkish baths were introduced in London. I think it was just after the Crimean War. Having tried them, and after making some inquiries about their construction, he proceeded to make one for himself at Alde House, his Aldeburgh home. It was a rough-and-ready affair, and I do not think it was very long-lived. A groom, not Barham, rubbing down a horse in the stable yard, was heard grumbling, "Master is buildin' hisself a sweatin' house : if he'd rub the hosses down he wouldn't want no sweatin' house."

He was extraordinarily helpful and generous in aiding young men in their first difficult steps towards a career. Many letters describing what the writers had owed to him in early life poured in upon my mother in the first weeks of her widowhood. But in this direction I think the most remarkable thing he ever did was to give active help and support to my sister Elizabeth, then aged about twenty, to enter the medical profession : at that time, of course, all the usual methods of entering the profession were not only closed, but barred, banged, and bolted against women. These bars and bolts a young, inexperienced girl, aided by her father, a country merchant, proposed to destroy and throw the gates open. My mother gave no help : she not only was unsympathetic, but intensely averse to the proposal. Sometimes he wavered, and would burst out to one of us, " I don't think I can go on with it, it will kill your mother " ; but it did not kill her, and her affectionate nature, aided by her strong practical common sense, in time reconciled her to seeing her daughter the pioneer in this great enterprise. When all the obstacles were at length overcome, and my sister an M.D. with her name upon the British register and very much held in honour by leading physicians and surgeons such as Sir James Paget and Sir T. Smith, and when Elizabeth (then Mrs. Anderson), as a member of the B.M.A., entertained the East Anglian branch at her house and garden at West Hill, Aldeburgh, none took part in the festival with more pleasure and graciousness than our dear mother.

She was an intensely religious woman, but all that side of her life, and the more real part of it, was a closed book to my father. His stumbling over the reading of family prayers must have been a constant thorn in her side. His idea was to make the necessary ceremony short : occasionally with this end in view he used to turn over two pages of the book of prayers instead of one : but this was apt to frustrate his object, for he might turn over the end of one prayer and land himself in the middle of another. When this happened, his resourcefulness stood him in good stead ; he would go on to a full stop, then pause and add, " For what we have received, the Lord make us truly thankful." My mother would rise from her knees pained and sad-looking ; but we irreverent children had mostly to bolt for the door so that our laughter should not further distress her. She worshipped my father, and admired him and everything about him. She was proud of his gift, for instance, in laying out grounds and gardens, and would say, " I can see it well enough when it is done ; but he can see it before it is begun." Devoted as she was to him, she took no part in his quarrels. One of his antagonists rushed out at her on some public occasion, and said, " Mrs. Garrett, I love you and all belonging to you, but your husband I will never forgive." She replied quite gently, " You will have to, Mr. ——, if you love all belonging to me, because he comes first of them all." I remember, too, at Christmas, when the usual gifts of the season were being prepared, her bringing her list to show him the names of those to whom she was sending turkeys, etc. He glanced over it, and exclaimed, " Why, don't you know I have quarrelled with that fellow ? " " Oh, yes, I know, father dear," she said, " but it don't matter." Thereupon he would leave her to do as she liked.

It was curious that my father and mother, though they

MY FATHER AND MOTHER IN THEIR OLD AGE.

From a photograph

To face page 34.

differed greatly from each other in character and outlook, each maintaining his or her own, almost wholly uninfluenced by the other, yet retained almost an awe of one another ; this was particularly evident in my father's case, as I can illustrate by an example. He and my sister Alice (Mrs. Cowell) took an excursion together in an Orient liner which was making a summer cruise in the Norwegian fjords. One Sunday morning the ship was lying in one of these, within full view of a village and its little church. My father expressed a wish to attend this church and hear the morning service. Alice acquiesced, and they were put ashore together. But the church was not so near as it had seemed to be from the deck of the liner, and there were other unforeseen difficulties in getting to it. However, nothing seemed to damp my father's determination to reach it, and presently Alice suggested that it was really of not very much consequence whether they reached it or not, because even if they did get there they would not be able to understand a single word of the service ; but my father rejoined at once, " Oh ! I know that, but I shall be able to tell your mother that I'd been." It was really he who bent to her more than she to him ; but neither of them had the least idea of the true state of the case.

My mother's religion was of the strict Evangelical type. She was a rigid Sabbatarian and read the *Record* and took in *Spurgeon's Sermons*. In theory, no doubt, she had no sympathy with the Roman custom of Prayers for the Dead ; but after my father's death she mentioned to us quite simply that as she had prayed for him every day for nearly sixty years of their life together she meant to go on praying for him now that death had parted them.

In domestic affairs she was orderly and methodical ; every department of her big household was well organized and thoroughly under her control. If such things had come her way, she would have proved a very capable organizer of a big business. But the management of her house and her correspondence with her ten children completely absorbed and satisfied her. She used to say with a happy smile, " The lines have fallen to me in pleasant places ; yea, I have a goodly heritage."

On my father's death, in May 1893, there was a passage about him in the *Aldeburgh Magazine*. It was anonymous, but I am practically certain that it was written by Canon Thompson, the very delightful man who succeeded Mr. Dowler as vicar of Aldeburgh. The writer speaks of Aldeburgh having lost a large-hearted and generous friend, and continued : " In Mr. Garrett a strong will and unfailing courage were added to a temperament almost overloaded with enthusiasm, energy, and activity. None of his virtues were passive. It may be supposed that this combination of qualities did not always in a small community make for peace, but below an occasionally stormy surface Mr. Garrett had a great heart, full of love for the town he had known so long and full of deep and kindly sympathy with his fellow-men. He was one in whom the instinct to help, when help was wanted, was unusually strong. Everyone in trouble turned to him, certain of aid if it could be given, and certain, too (even when in fault), of generous judgment."

Ten years after this, in January 1903, on the death of our dear mother, Canon Thompson wrote these lines to my brother Edmund :

THE VICARAGE,
Second Sunday after the Epiphany, 1903.

MY DEAR MR. GARRETT,

I write a few words, not because of your need to be told how we honour and love your dear mother, but because it soothes my sorrow to dwell a moment thus upon her worth. For in sorrow we most sincerely are : we feel that in our second degree we, too, have lost a mother. Such she ever showed herself to us ; in spite of the unusually wide circle of interests she had, she always found room in her large heart for our interests—joyful or painful. . . . I used to seek her counsel not only because she was a wise woman, as she was, but more because she sought her counsel from God. Many will miss her kindness, but I think a greater loss will be her goodness, her holiness; of that we shall have the memory, but no more the pattern, before our eyes. A more consistent Christian I never knew, and I love to recall the downrightness with which she used to say and write what she thought, all the while accusing herself, dear soul, of not confessing herself as she ought. As for my ministrations to her, I used to go to her feeling I wanted help and could get it, not that I carried it. If I did not feel that we should still have her prayers, I should feel the loss irreparable. These things I write —not in depreciation of those who are to take her place, but in sympathy with the thoughts which I am sure are in their hearts as they take up their duties.

You can show this to anyone who you would like to see it; I want the family to know how thankful we are for the inspiration of such a life and death.

Believe me, ever yours sincerely,
HENRY THOMPSON.

Chapter IV

MISS BROWNING'S SCHOOL AT BLACKHEATH AND WHAT GREW OUT OF IT

I AND ALL MY SISTERS but the youngest were sent in turn to a school at Blackheath presided over by Miss Louisa Browning. She was an aunt of the poet and a remarkable person in many ways. She ruled her school with a rod of iron ; but she was a born teacher, and we all appreciated her thoroughness and method, especially as our ancient governess at home had been incompetent to the last degree. One of Miss Browning's peculiarities was an objection to needlework in her school. This, she considered, ought to have been taught to us at home. If she saw a girl with a needle in her hand, she would call out in her most commanding tones, " A guinea a stitch, my dear, a guinea a stitch ! " Another peculiarity was her passion for gay colours. She daringly mingled scarlet, purple, green, and yellow on her ample person. I remember being taken to school by my father after the summer holidays in 1861, a week or two after the death of Elizabeth Barrett Browning, and Miss Browning's entry into the little drawing-room, clad, as usual, in all the colours of the rainbow. After the more formal greetings, she said to my father, " No doubt, Mr. Garrett, you are astonished not to find me in mourning ; but I have a black dress upstairs in case Robert should call." I never heard that Robert did call, nor saw anything of the black dress ; but in after-years, in books and articles written about Robert Browning and his family, I have met with passages some of which asserted positively that he was a Jew by birth, while others denied it. I cannot bring any positive knowledge to bear on the point. Our Miss Browning had an elder brother named Reuben, but this does not prove anything. There was a Richard Garrett, my father's great-grand-father (born 1733, died 1787), who had ten sons, three of whom were named respectively Abraham, Isaac, and Jacob ; but we have every reason to believe that he was of an unmixed East Anglian stock, and had no trace of Jewish blood. Miss Browning used to talk to us sometimes about her brothers. Reuben, she declared, was a very devout Christian, but the most selfish man she had ever met, while her darling youngest brother not only was not a professed Christian, but had no religion at all, nothing but the dearest, kindest heart in the world. I have sometimes reflected, especially since I have had the opportunity of seeing Palestine, Algeria, Egypt, etc., that possibly Miss Browning's love of bright-coloured clothing may indicate an Eastern strain in her ancestry ; but she had a very British look.

When my elder sisters, Louie and Elizabeth, were at Blackheath, they had among their schoolfellows two very charming North Country girls, Sophie and Annie Crowe. Their home was at Usworth, in the county of Durham, and my sisters more than once spent part of their summer holidays there. On one of these visits they were introduced to Miss Emily Davies, the only daughter of the Rev. Dr. Davies, rector of Gates-head. The friendship this formed between my sisters, the Crowes, and Miss Davies lasted as long as their lives, and had a strong and enduring influence, not only on the little group immediately concerned, but also on nearly the whole of my family.

Miss Davies had a strong and masterful character ; she had early in her own life set before herself as a definite object the improvement of the whole social and political status of women.   I do not know how far, if at all, her mind had been influenced by those of her own way of thinking who had preceded her, such as Mary Woll-stonecraft, Godwin, and the Shelleys.   I think probably not at all, except in so far as these pioneers indicated to her the way not to do it.   Miss Davies was the least revolutionary of revolutionists.   She meant to spell revolution without the *r*.   She wanted women to have as good and thorough an education as men ; she wanted to open the professions to them and to obtain for them the Parliamentary franchise.   But she did not want any violence either of speech or action.   She remained always the quiet, demure little rector's daughter, and she meant to bring about all the changes she advocated by processes as gradual and unceasing as the progress of a child from infancy to manhood.   Her best route towards her ultimate goal was, she was convinced, through education, and this for a double reason.   Firstly, improved education for women was good in itself and would arouse the minimum of opposition.   Secondly, education was a necessary preliminary to enable women to occupy the place in national life at which Miss Davies aimed for them.   Mrs. Somerville, Miss Herschel, Miss Martineau, and Mrs. Fry had already done really fine work in their several lines, and they were all women who from various accidental circumstances had received a first-rate education.   That which had qualified them for their work, Miss Davies aimed at securing for women at large.   She was pre-eminently one of those reformers who saw the end from the beginning.   She had a logical, thorough, and far-seeing mind ; delicately scrupulous as to methods, honest and truthful in word and deed, and also unswerving and unceasing as to objects. She obtained a strong influence over my two elder sisters, and through them a little later on the rest of us. She did not influence my sister Agnes and myself in our childhood. She had had no younger brothers or sisters of her own (her only brother, the Rev. J. Llewellyn Davies, was nearly of her own age), and her manner towards us was not winning. She always seemed (I am speaking still of the late 'fifties and early 'sixties) to be letting us know of how little consequence we were. Later, especially when her experience as first Principal of Girton College had brought her more into contact with young people, her manner softened and she became the friend and comrade of our adult life rather than the stern preceptor of our youth. In 1857 our eldest sister, Louie, married. Alice, our third sister, also married a few years later. Her husband, Herbert Cowell, was practising law in Calcutta, where she spent nearly ten years. Elizabeth consequently became more than ever, therefore, the leader and friend of the younger half of the family. Her deep fund of natural human affection and almost maternal feeling towards us prevented her from falling into the mannerisms which for a time estranged us from Miss Davies. One of Elizabeth's inventions for our benefit was what she called *Talks on Things in General*, which took place on Sunday evenings. I can see her now on the sofa in the Alde House drawing-room : George, our youngest brother, on her lap, and the rest of us grouped round her while she talked on just what was uppermost in her own mind at the time : Garibaldi and the freeing of Italy from the Austrians, Carlyle's *Cromwell*, Macaulay's *History of England*, and modern political events and persons, such as Lord Palmerston, and the chances of a Reform Bill, Louis Napoleon and the Haynau incident, etc., etc.

I remember taking the most lively interest in the 1857 campaign in Italy against the Austrians, when the French joined forces with the King of Sardinia. From that time Garibaldi, Cavour, and Victor Emmanuel became my heroes, and I tried to learn all I could about them. To show what a queer little creature I was at that time, I may mention that I remember thinking on my tenth birthday that I had now reached the prime of life and that henceforward I must expect a descent towards the sere and yellow leaf of old age. Perhaps this temperament may explain why Miss Davies wished to snub me. Several years later I was telling my brother George my childish notion of ten being the prime of life, and he in return told me of one of his blunders when he was about the same age. He had begun making a small collection of coins, and was familiar with the terms " obverse " and " reverse " as applied to them. One Sunday in church the hymn selected contained the lines :

> Oh, my spirit longs and faints
> For the converse of the saints.

He thought this was an example of the extraordinary ideas grown-ups had of enjoying themselves. He had mixed up the word " converse " with " obverse " and " reverse," and thought the hymn indicated an uncontrollable desire to turn the saints upside down or inside out. Probably everyone who remembers his childhood will recall similar grotesque mistakes.

One of my great joys while at Blackheath was to come up for an occasional week-end with my sister Louie, then living in Manchester Square. She was thirteen years older than myself, and was almost as much a mother to me as a sister. It was she who first opened to me the beauty and wisdom of Wordsworth's poetry, beginning with the Tintern Abbey poem, " The Happy Warrior," and the Ode on the " Intimations of Immortality." There are some lines from these which I always associate with her and with our walks together in Kensington Gardens. On these week-end visits Louie and her husband usually took me to some fascinating entertainment on Saturday afternoon or evening, and on Sunday to hear the Rev. F. D. Maurice preach at St. Peter's, Vere Street. On Monday morning early I was escorted to an omnibus at the Marble Arch, which deposited me at London Bridge station for the train to Greenwich, whence I walked to my school at Blackheath. My reason for recalling these small excursions now is that many times as my omnibus passed Newgate on Monday morning I saw the huge crowd of evil-looking people assembled outside the prison in order to enjoy the recreation of seeing a man hanged. These executions were then carried out in public, and I cannot imagine a more degrading exhibition. Boys whom we knew at St. Paul's School (then situated close to Newgate) told us that nothing was done by the school authorities to prevent the lads witnessing the executions. They themselves, they said, thought nothing of going to see them. Public executions were not abolished until 1867. " Sporting " young men of quite good position used to look upon attendance at an execution as quite a legitimate way of enjoying themselves, and I remember one of my Leiston cousins driving himself the forty odd miles to Norwich to see a notorious murderer hanged. These things measure in some degree the distance between 1860 and 1923.

Another feature of my week-ends, in strange contrast with the Newgate horrors, was hearing a great leader of religious thought deliver his soul on the theological problems which were then agitating men's minds. It was the period just preceding the publication of *Essays and Reviews* and the prosecution of Bishop Colenso for heresy ; and masses of devoutly religious people were clinging tenaciously to the theory that every word in the Bible was verbally inspired by God Himself and therefore must be true, while modern science, even modern common sense, showed plainly that this could not be so. For instance, though the Pentateuch says that the hare chews the cud, it is common knowledge now that the hare does not chew the cud. It was Maurice's intense conviction which penetrated all his teaching that the spirit of man seeking approach to his Maker was not to be deterred by the proven fact that human error in matters of science formed part of the Bible. It would have been a miracle had it been otherwise. It mattered not an iota to a seeker after the Spirit of God whether the hare chewed the cud or not. The spirit answers to the spirit and the flesh to the flesh. This is not the place to discuss such problems as these, but I hold myself fortunate to have heard Maurice repeatedly at a time when my own mind was in process of formation. He had the voice, the look, the inspiration of a prophet ; and spiritual things were to him the greatest realities in the universe.

At Aldeburgh and at Snape, where I had " sat under " Mr. Dowler, a pure formalist and a dull one at that, and Mr. Baker, a most amusing Irishman, I had never heard a word bearing on these problems. Mr. Dowler was platitudinous to the last degree : he never failed on each first Sunday of the month to say " but as we must be brief on this our Sacrament morning." We hailed the brevity and escaped out of church glad to have got it over in a shorter time than usual. At Snape Church we were continually on the watch for Mr. Baker's amusing eccentricities. He had a way of interpolating little remarks of his own into the Lessons or Psalms of the day, or, indeed, in any other part of the service. For instance, he would read in his rich rolling Irish voice, " The people who sat in darkness (that was their state) sora great light (that was a better state) " ; to the words " King of Kings, Lord of Lords," he once added, " There's a many sort of lords : Lord Rendlesham ! What is he ? Nothing but a poorr, earrthly worrum ; that's not the Lord we have here." Once well in the middle of the Nicene Creed he paused and exclaimed, " Stop, stop, stop ! I've forgot the Holy Gospel "—this in his ordinary secular voice—and then without an instant's pause adding in his clerical voice, " The Holy Gospel is written in the ninth chapter of that according to Saint Matthew, beginning at the fourteenth verse."

As these are actual literal transcripts from the pastors and masters who had represented the Church of England to my childhood, it is no wonder that both heart and mind were arrested and impressed by F. D. Maurice, who seemed to me to be a modern Isaiah. He awakened in me new thoughts and, I hope, partially at all events, new reverences.

It is only fair to add here that Canon Thompson, who succeeded Mr. Dowler as vicar of Aldeburgh, was a type of the very best kind of clergyman, devout, thoughtful, and original both in his thoughts and in his method of expressing them ; but he did not come to Aldeburgh until long after the time of which I am now writing.

I have already referred to the more serious side of Canon Thompson's character : but I should like also to show another facet of his mind ; he had a strong sense of humour kept under strict control. One of his curates, Mr. Brook, also had a sense of humour, but from the clerical point of view not adequately controlled. Canon Thompson said to one of us, " I dare not mention even the slightest jest to Brook in the vestry : he has such a terribly loud laugh ! " Canon Thompson did not laugh : he only smiled. One Sunday, when I was on a visit to Alde House, Canon Thompson's sermon was about a Church in Asia to which one of St. Paul's epistles had been addressed. He said : " It was a very small Church, and it was insignificant in another respect : it was almost entirely composed of women." I flamed with indignation at this : but my mother's presence made me control myself. But there seems to have been a brain-wave which conveyed my sentiments to the pulpit, for the Canon immediately added, " But let us not think less of it for that ! What would the Christian Church be without its women ?—their purity of motive, their unselfish enthusiasm, their good works ? " etc., etc. I was placated, but not satisfied ; and a day or two after, when he was calling on my mother, I felt he had been delivered into my hands, and said, " I nearly called out ' Shame ' in the middle of your sermon last Sunday, Canon Thompson." He at once replied with his most demure clerical manner, " I know what you mean, but I made it up to you afterwards, didn't I ? "

I will give one more story to illustrate his humour and his observation. There was a travelling dramatic company playing in Aldeburgh, and my sister, Mrs. Anderson, engaged them to perform *As You Like It* in her garden : all Aldeburgh, including the Vicar and his wife, were present. He sat with an abstracted look on his face, so that it was difficult to say whether his mind was not a thousand leagues away. The actress who played Rosalind was a lady of very ample proportions, with enormous arms, bare to her shoulder, and as large in circumference as a good-sized tree. The next day this poor lady came to see my sister to pour into her ear details of a misfortune which had befallen her. Her husband, who had played the exiled Duke, had run away from her, taking with him not only his own salary, but also hers ! What could she do ? After a good deal of talk, my sister thought she would like to consult the Vicar. She found him and told him all the sad story. He listened with great attention, and then said very solemnly, "What? Left her? Fled? From those arms?" But, of course, he did not fail to help the poor woman.

Chapter V

OUR DERBYSHIRE COUSINS
AND OTHER FRIENDS

WHEN I WENT BACK TO SCHOOL without my sister Agnes I might have felt very lonely and bereft if it had not been that now for the first time I had as chief friend and companion my cousin, several times removed according to genealogy, but most closely allied in friendship, Rhoda Garrett. Rhoda's father, the Rev. John Fisher Garrett, rector of Elton in Derbyshire, was grandson of the Richard Garrett, already mentioned, who died in 1787, leaving ten sons ; my father being his great-grandson. Therefore the relationship was not very close. But that is the best of cousins, you can make much or little of the relationship, according to your taste and fancy ; in Rhoda's case it meant much, especially to Agnes and myself. Rhoda was a little older than we were, of brilliant capacity and great personal attractiveness, witty and very ready with her wit. Her mother had died in her early childhood, and after several years of widowhood her father had married again, and a fairly rapid succession of babies appeared once more in the Elton Rectory. The three children of the first marriage were almost by force of circumstances pushed out of the parent nest. One son went to New Zealand and stayed there ; one was in an office in London ; and it became a question what should Rhoda do ? At that time governessing was practically the only professional career open to a woman. My eldest sister, Louie (Mrs. Smith), determined that if Rhoda had to be a governess she should at least have some preparation for her work, and sent her to Gebweiler, in Alsace, where she could learn both French and German ; after a course of instruction there, she came for further tuition in English subjects to Miss Browning's school at Blackheath. She immediately became my guide, philosopher and friend, and more particularly my protector, if she thought there was anything in the school management that was not satisfactory so far as I was concerned. She was far more ready than I was to perceive occasions for her active intervention. I might even have resented her aid if it had not been that she had such a pleasant way with her that it was impossible to take offence or to withstand her.[1]

Our school friendship, and especially that which Rhoda formed with Agnes, almost at the same time had important consequences. After my marriage, in 1867, Rhoda and Agnes determined to live together and get themselves trained as house-decorators, a thing quite as unprecedented then as women becoming doctors. Rhoda also took an active part in the agitation led by Mrs. Butler against the Contagious Diseases Acts of 1866 and 1868 and in working for Women's Suffrage. She became a speaker of extraordinary power and eloquence. Many of her hearers declared her to be quite unequalled for her combination of humour with logic and closely reasoned argument. Sometimes the newspaper comments were very droll. One which sticks in my memory ran thus : " The lecturer, who wore no hat, was youthful *but* composed, feminine *but* intelligent."

One of the Elton Rectory babies, Fydell Edmund Garrett, Rhoda's half-brother, distinguished himself

[1] A very vivid picture of Rhoda is given in Dame Ethel Smyth's *Impressions Which Remain.*

greatly in after-life, becoming a real power in the troubled political waters of South Africa, Member of the Cape Parliament, and the very brilliant editor of the *Cape Times*. His life was written by his friend, the late Sir Edward Cook, so I will dwell no further upon it here, except to say that he possessed from his childhood the gifts of personal charm and personal beauty. He was greatly loved by us all, and one of the things we like to remember is that Rhodes, on one occasion when he was reckoning up the assets of South Africa, said, " Well, you see, there's myself and Milner and Garrett."

But to go back to Miss Browning's school. It changed hands before I left it, but I again had the good fortune to be in the charge of a really competent teacher who was extremely good to me and to whom I was devoted. My school-days, however, were brought abruptly to an end before I was sixteen. From causes which I imperfectly understood, there was suddenly a financial crisis at home. I suppose that my father's speculative and courageous temperament had brought difficulties upon him, and that a sort of Geddes axe of stringent economy had to be applied to his domestic expenditure. I was bitterly sorry to leave school ; but my parents were very good in making it up to me as well as they could by allowing me undisturbed use of our old schoolroom for reading and study in the mornings. The financial difficulties, whatever they were, were not long-lived, as the brother next younger than myself, Sam, was presently sent to Rugby and afterwards to Cambridge ; and, of course, there were plenty of opportunities for me to enjoy my home life, diversified as it was by riding, dancing, skating, walking, and boating on the Alde. So I did not regard myself as a martyr, though I did miss the good teaching I had had at Blackheath. I had a little bedroom to myself, and there I stored my favourite books, including a huge volume containing all Shakespeare's plays (not the sonnets, which were a later discovery)—this my schoolfellows had given me as a parting present. I spent many Sunday afternoons with this beloved book, laughing over Benedick and Beatrice and weeping over Desdemona, though I was angry with her for allowing Othello to kill her when she ought to have known what anguish it would be to him after he had found out his atrocious blunder.

We all followed with keen interest my sister Elizabeth's struggle to get her name inscribed on the British Medical Register, and sympathized with her in her absolute rejection of anything which would-be friends recommended as "just as good"; for her acceptance of this advice would have consigned women to a lower rank in the profession than that open to men.

We had from time to time delightful visits to London, where, in addition to dances, which we loved, we were taken to the opera for the first time and drank deep of the delights of glorious music. In this connection I must confess to a piece of wanton cruelty on our part : we made our Uncle Balls, our father's brother, take us to a philharmonic concert. He asked us, kind old man, what we should like by way of a treat, and that was our choice, quite regardless of his feelings, for he cared no more for music than a mastodon would have done. How he bore it I cannot tell, but we enjoyed it hugely ; there for the first time we heard Haydn's quartet, the one which introduces the famous Hymn to the Emperor, from the time of its composition until 1918 the Austrian National Anthem.

In 1865 I was taken by my sister Louie and her husband to one of J. S. Mill's election meetings. It will be remembered that from the moment of his being invited to become a candidate for the historic borough he had made it quite clear that he attached the greatest importance to the political enfranchisement of women. This alienated some supporters, but attracted others, among them my brother-in-law, who was an elector. It was the first time that women's suffrage had been brought before English electors as a practical question, and in 1865 there was no country in the world which had adopted it. The room where the meeting was held was not large, but it was densely crowded. I do not remember Mill's speech, but I do remember the impression made by his delicate, sensitive physique, united as it was with a very unusual degree of moral courage. I also remember very distinctly that when the heckling began a man rose in the audience and said he had a question to ask. He then proceeded to read a passage from a book in his hand, in which the statement was made that the characteristic fault of the British working man was untruthfulness. The heckler then personally addressed Mr. Mill and said, " The question I wish to ask is, did you write this ? " Mill instantly rose and simply said, " I did," and sat down again. The effect was instantaneous and electrical. The meeting cheered itself hoarse. Mill's candour and directness were such a delightful contrast to the usual shiftiness of Parliamentary candidates. His personality added to the effect he produced ; and I heard it stated afterwards that those two words, " I did," won him the election. He was, of course, a staunch upholder of an extended franchise which should include the then voteless masses of working men and also women. I was a woman suffragist, I may say, from my cradle, but this meeting kindled tenfold my enthusiasm for it. The time of which I am now writing covered the years of the American Civil War. I, following my sister Elizabeth, was a staunch Northerner, and I studied all the arguments carefully which sought to prove that the question of slavery was the real cause of the war.

This was not so clear and obvious as it became as the war went on. Lincoln, in his inaugural address as President in March 1861, had said, " We had no purpose directly or indirectly to interfere with the institution of slavery in the States where it exists." It is not unnatural that this was misunderstood in England and represented as meaning that Lincoln, to say the least, was half-hearted in his opposition to slavery. We did not understand then, as well as we have been taught to do since, the series of checks and limitations which surround the great powers of the President of the United States. Lincoln's power as President was limited, as he himself expressed it, to seeing that the laws of the Union were faithfully executed in all the States. When civil war broke out Lincoln became the Commander-in-Chief of the Army, and in that capacity he issued, on 1st January 1863, the Proclamation definitely abolishing slavery in the rebel States. This was done by him as an act of war. These controversies are dead now that the whole of the facts are known, but they were very much alive at the time which I am endeavouring to recall. Then, early in 1865, came in rapid succession the carrying of the thirteenth amendment to the American Constitution abolishing for ever by constitutional machinery the institution of slavery in the U.S.A. ; the final collapse of the Southern Army with the surrender of its noble leader, R. E. Lee, on 9th April ; and on 14th April the assassination of the greatest man the North has ever produced, Abraham Lincoln.

I have recited all this rather in detail because of the influence these events had on my life. I was staying with Louie in London, and we were invited on the very day the news of the murder of Lincoln reached England to a party at Aubrey House, Campden Hill, the residence of Mr. P. A. Taylor, M.P., and his wife. They were both ardent Northerners, and represented the left wing of the party of political and social reform at that time. My future husband was there. I had heard of him ; of his blindness, and of his heroic courage in overcoming its drawbacks, but till that evening I had never seen him. When we arrived at the party there was a great buzz of excited conversation, in which I joined, about the tragedy of Lincoln's death. I was not yet quite eighteen, but the phrase "We are none of us omniscient, not even the youngest," had not then been coined ; so I expressed what I felt without hesitation and said that the death of Lincoln was the greatest misfortune which could have befallen the world from the loss of any one man. Challenged to particularize what I meant, I added, " Yes, greater than the loss of any of the crowned heads in Europe." There was nothing but what was obvious in this ; but the expression struck the ears of the blind man who, some two years later, became my husband. I was told many years afterwards that he had immediately asked Mrs. Peter Taylor to introduce him to me. In any case he kept them in his memory, cultivated the acquaintance of my father and sister when he met them at the British Association or elsewhere, and in 1866 accepted an invitation from my father to come down and spend a few days at Alde House. That settled my future life ; we became engaged in October 1866, and were married in 1867 on St. George's Day, which was also the day of Shakespeare's and Wordsworth's birth ; and in future years the day of the breaking of the Zeebrugge mole in 1918. Therefore it is, of all the days in the year, my favourite.

Chapter VI

MY MARRIAGE AND NEW HOMES IN LONDON AND SALISBURY, 1867–1884

M Y MARRIAGE naturally made an enormous difference in my life, an even greater difference than is usual in the normal cases of the passage from girlhood to wife and motherhood. From the quietest of quiet country life I was transplanted into a society of surpassing interest and novelty both in London and Cambridge. My husband was in Parliament, and a conspicuous figure there even from the first. He was also a Professor of the University of Cambridge. We had a small settled income, and upon that had to maintain two homes, one in London and the other at Cambridge. It was a tight fit, but it could be done, and was done without any Spartan privations. I was a dragon over every unnecessary expenditure ; for I was a firm believer in Mr. Micawber's receipt for producing either happiness or misery.

My husband, notwithstanding his blindness, had a keen enjoyment of life and all its ordinary occupations, sports and interests. He skated, rode, and went to Scotland on fishing expeditions most autumns ; we dined with our friends and gave them little dinners in return. The secretary he had had before his marriage (Edward Brown) left him in 1867 ; he had a boy who was careful and conscientious in leading him about, to and from the House, when we were in London, and to his lectures, etc., when we were in Cambridge, but this well-disposed and kindly lad had neither the education nor the capacity to be of much other service to him. Once, when my husband had to make a railway journey from Cambridge into East Suffolk to vote at a bye-election (my father had given him a tiny freehold as a qualification), Harry and his young secretary had to travel many hours in bad cross-country trains in order to get the double journey over in a day. To the lad it was an unprecedented treat to spend so many hours in first-class carriages ; but a misfortune befel him : in putting his head out of the window when the train was in motion his hat blew off. Harry deeply sympathized, and telegraphed from the next stopping-place about the lost treasure. " How shall I describe it, my boy ? " said he. The reply was, " Please say, sir, it was quite new and rather fashionable." My husband's huge enjoyment of this is an illustration of his temperament which carried him for the most part light-heartedly over the inevitable privations of blindness.

His many friends in Cambridge, and his devoted parents and sister at Salisbury, provided him with another unfailing source of strength and good cheer. It has often been told that when out partridge shooting a misdirected shot from his father's gun had cost him his eyesight. The anguish of a very loving father can hardly be imagined ; but it roused in the son a settled determination to make his father see that the misfortune had not blighted the life so dear to him.

I received a most generous and loving welcome into this home circle, and I cannot speak with sufficient reverence and gratitude of my sister-in-law, Maria Fawcett. From the time of the accident, until our marriage, she had been all in all to her brother, lavishing on him her great love and watchful care : now, when I appeared, suddenly, to her, upon the scene, she did not look upon me as a supplanter, but welcomed me as a comrade and friend. I have never known a nobler or more generous nature. She was so full of loving appreciation, there was no room in her heart for jealousy or suspicion.

Mr. F. J. Dryhurst did not become my husband's private secretary until 1871. He was from that time invaluable, and became a most faithful and lifelong friend. He was introduced to us by the Rev. J. Llewellyn Davies, who had known him from boyhood.

My husband's father was a North Country man, born at Kirkby Lonsdale in 1793. He was fishing under the beautiful bridge at Kirkby in 1805 when he heard of the Battle of Trafalgar and the death of Nelson. He was an only son, his parents died young, and he migrated in early youth to the South of England, first to London and then to Salisbury. He was in London in 1814, and attended the gala performance of the opera given in that year to welcome the Allied Sovereigns who were rather prematurely celebrating their victory over Napoleon ; then came the escape from Elba, the hundred days and the short campaign which ended triumphantly at Waterloo. All this Mr. Fawcett remembered perfectly, and it was extraordinarily interesting to hear of these great events from him. He had settled in Salisbury before 1815, and he used to tell us of seeing from a distance the coach arriving from London decorated with branches of laurel. This was the method of telegraphing a victory, and when the coach finally pulled up in the Salisbury market-place he was the one deputed to jump on the top and read the dispatch announcing details of the triumph to the assembled crowd ; for his ringing North Country voice carried farther than the Wiltshire gutturals. About 1828 he married a Salisbury lady, Mary Cooper, daughter of a solicitor. He had joined the volunteers that were raised while the

campaign was at its height, was a member of the Salisbury
Corporation a little later, became Mayor in 1832, the
year of the first Reform Bill. He was a good judge
of both food and wine ; and living, as he did, to extreme
old age (ninety-five), one of the cathedral dignitaries,
a feeble old gentleman with an impaired digestion, had
the happy thought of consulting my father-in-law as
to daily diet : " I suppose, Mr. Fawcett," he said,
" you have always been an extremely abstemious man,
especially in the matter of wine ? " The reply was
emphatic : " I have never said ' No ' to a good glass of
wine in m' life." On another occasion another ecclesi-
astic adopted another plan ; he asked no advice, but he
sat facing Mr. Fawcett at a municipal banquet, and
watching every dish and every wine of which my father-
in-law partook, took exactly the same himself. His
wife had to send for a doctor in the middle of the night,
as the unfortunate man thought his end was approaching.
But let none imagine that these anecdotes indicate that
my father-in-law was anything but a most temperate
man ; he had a fine palate, and enjoyed good wine
and good food all the more for his moderation in
their use.

Mrs. Fawcett, my husband's mother, was a very able
and capable woman : she wrote excellent letters, as she
had an intuitive sense of what her correspondent was
interested in and wanted to hear. She loved to know
all she could about her neighbours, and to pass on her
information. She was a keen politician, and delighted
to dwell on her friendship, during the anti-corn law campaign, with Bright and Cobden ; her Liberalism was on
strictly party lines : whatever " the Party " ordained, she
automatically became a strong supporter of. During
the time I knew her she never gave an ounce of sympathy
to any cause before " the Party " had done so : there
were, as in most country towns, rigidly defined political

barriers between the shops in the city—Liberal drapers, fishmongers, and so on, and Tory drapers, fishmongers, and so on. Mrs. Fawcett would never have dreamed of going into any but those in sympathy with the Liberals. I remember her indignation with me on one occasion because I had shown myself more intent on getting what I wanted than on inquiring into the politics of the shop in which I found it. But she was extremely good to me and patient in bearing with our differences in outlook. Another tie between us was that she had a keen sense of humour which never failed her. Almost the only time I remember her being seriously angry with me was on account of my having spoken during a bye-election in Southwark in 1870 on behalf of Mr. George Odger, a Labour candidate,[1] at a time when the Labour Party had not come into existence.

It was not that Mrs. Fawcett disapproved of Odger's politics or character. She did not care enough about him to inquire into either: nor did she express disapproval of my husband appearing on his platform and speaking and working for him. But at that time it was an unheard-of thing for women to speak on election plat-forms, and that I had done this on behalf of a candidate who was in opposition to the Liberal Party was to her almost an unforgivable sin. I couldn't promise I would never do it again, but I did promise never to speak in Salisbury unless she invited me to do so, and this promise, of course, I kept, and in course of time she did invite me and I accepted the invitation.

Two of the most interesting inhabitants of Salisbury at the time of my marriage were Dr. and Mrs. Fowler. He was a retired physician, and in his young days had formed a part of the Holland House group of Whigs. He brought to Salisbury anecdotes of the Holland House

---

[1] See Mr. F. W. Soutter's book, *Recollections of a Labour Pioneer*. T. Fisher Unwin, 1922.

dinner parties and of Lady Holland's management of her guests : Macaulay was, of course, very frequently one of them, and dominated the rest of the company by his encyclopædic knowledge and his facility in pouring it forth. On one of these occasions, when for a long time there had not been one brilliant flash of silence, Lady Holland beckoned to a footman, and said to him, " Go round to Mr. Macaulay, and say ' that'll do.' "

Mrs. Fowler was a lady quite of the old school. She had in her childhood sat on the knee of Dr. Johnson, and it interested us to observe how few links were necessary to fill up the 150 years or so which covered the time between our little daughter and Queen Anne. Philippa had been patted on the head by Mrs. Fowler, who had sat on the knee of Dr. Johnson, who had been " touched " by Queen Anne.

Another very warm Salisbury friend was Dr. Roberts, also a retired physician. He sympathized with my husband's general outlook in politics, and they had other interests in common. We used to drive out occasionally in Dr. Roberts's company to dine with Dr. and Mrs. Roland Williams, the former then being rector of Broadchalke. He was rather frowned upon by the " County " and the Cathedral dignitaries of Salisbury for having written one of the articles in the once famous *Essays and Reviews*. The charming old rectory at Broadchalke was afterwards acquired by the late Mr. Maurice Hewlett, who created a marvellous series of gardens round it.

During the months of the Parliamentary Session which we spent in London, I regarded it as a very great honour when we were invited from time to time to dine with Mr. Mill and his stepdaughter, Miss Helen Taylor, at Blackheath. These were delightful evenings, when we met Mr. and Mrs. Grote, Professor Cairnes, Herbert Spencer, and other celebrities, and heard, I suppose, some of the best talk from some of the best talkers in England. Of course questions concerning Women's Suffrage and the general position of women not infrequently came up, and I remember a discussion between Mill and Herbert Spencer, the latter taking the " anti " line, and basing his arguments on the heavy handicap nature had imposed upon women.

Mill's reply took my fancy exceedingly. He said, " You look upon nature as something we should do well to follow. I look upon nature as a horrible old harridan." Again, it was interesting to hear Mrs. Grote explaining why she had become a suffragist. She always reminded me of a well-bred old country gentleman ; tall, robust, and well set up in every way, towering over her rather delicate finicking-looking husband, who resembled a Dresden China figure. Mrs. Grote habitually spoke and wrote of him as " the Historian." When anything was said which surprised her she would exclaim, " Good God, good God, you astound me." When explaining to us what made her a suffragist, she said, " When I discovered that the purse in my pocket and the watch at my side were not my own, but the Historian's, I felt it was time women should have the power to amend these preposterous laws." However, of course the laws went on unamended for many years after this. I have related elsewhere [1] how at a Liberal meeting at my father's house in Suffolk I had taken round a petition asking Parliament to pass the Married Women's Property Bill then before it. Those present were mostly Suffolk farmers ; I explained my petition and asked for signatures but obtained very few. One old farmer voiced the feelings of the majority. " Am I to understand you, ma'am, that if this Bill becomes law and my wife had a matter of a hundred pound left her, I should have

[1] See *Women's Suffrage: a Short History of a Great Movement*, T. C. and E. C. Jack.

to *arst* her for it ? " Of course I was obliged to confess
that he would have to suffer this humiliation, and then
I got no more signatures.

It was several years after this, I believe in 1877, that
I had another illustration of this monstrous state of the
law. I was at Waterloo station taking a ticket ; as
I dropped my purse back into my pocket I felt a hand
there that was not my own. I naturally grabbed it
and tried to hold it ; naturally, also, I was unsuccessful ;
it belonged to a young man who quickly broke from me
with my purse in his possession. Some bystanders
grasped the situation and pursued the thief, who threw
my purse on the ground, and his flight was ended in
the arms of a policeman. He and the thief and I were
then marched off to a small office in the station, where
there was a police inspector. The policeman said,
" This here young gen'leman have been liftin' a bit off
the person of this here young lady." The Inspector
said to me, " Do you charge him ? " and I replied,
" Yes." If I had known then as much as I knew later,
I should have said " No," and contented myself with
the recovery of my purse. " But I, being young and
foolish," did not see that this would have been the best
both for me and for the thief. He was brought up
before a police magistrate the next day and committed
for trial at the Surrey Sessions. I had to come up from
Cambridge in about six weeks' time to give evidence
against him. When in the court I saw the charge
sheet, and noted that the thief was charged with
" stealing from the person of Millicent Fawcett a purse
containing £1 18s. 6d., the property of Henry Fawcett."
I felt as if I had been charged with theft myself. A few
minutes later I heard my thief condemned to seven
years' penal servitude, a very terrible thing for him,
almost a sentence of death, at any rate, of social and
industrial death. I am a magistrate myself now, and

I often watch with respectful admiration the humanity and wisdom with which the presiding magistrate at the Newington Sessions, Sir Robert Wallace, deals with cases, now infrequent, of this kind ; always trying through the probation system to give offenders, especially young offenders, another chance to come back into respectable methods of getting a living. It seems to me that the pessimists are altogether wrong, that the world is better and not worse than it was fifty years ago, more intelligent and more humane, and that the results of the comparatively gentle method of dealing with crime have not increased it, but the contrary. If I may refer here to another little piece of my small magisterial experience, I may mention having sat occasionally over a period of some three years as a member of the Holborn Bench to hear education summonses. My colleague in this capacity not infrequently was the late Sir John Kirk, one of the founders with Lord Shaftesbury of the Ragged School Union movement. This dear gentle old Christian gentleman was moved with compassion not only for the defaulting parents, but also for me, inexperienced as I was in the more seamy side of the life of the London poor, by the evidence brought before us of their wretchedness, as one after another a bedraggled and sodden-looking woman with one baby in her arms, another pulling at her skirts, was brought before us and called upon to explain why her son or daughter under the age of fourteen had not punctually attended school. Sir John Kirk used to say to me in a low voice so that no one but myself should hear him, " You must not let these things make you too unhappy. These that come before us are the failures ; but the great mass is *very satisfactory indeed.*" The way he used to explain to parents how they could get helped, that there was a Care Committee which would aid them materially if applied to and that the whole machinery of the Court was devised in order to help them, and especially their children, to make good in the world and have a fair chance of a more satisfactory existence in the future, made a deep impression on me and was a lesson how these magisterial duties should be performed.

But I must go back to the time immediately after my marriage. My political education was just beginning ; naturally I had to read and write for my husband. I grappled with newspapers and blue books, and learned more or less to convey their import to him. He took care that I should hear important debates in the House of Commons, and the Speaker and Serjeant-at-Arms were very kind in frequently offering me a seat in that portion of the ladies' galleries which they controlled. Of course, the heavy brass trellis which then screened off these galleries, and their bad ventilation, made them quite unnecessarily tiring and even exhausting ; but the whole scene was new to me and very interesting. During the debates on the Reform Bill of 1867 I heard the famous speech of Disraeli when, replying to a vehement personal onslaught from Gladstone, he had said that he had congratulated himself that he had been protected from his adversary by the substantial piece of furniture which lay between them. These chaffing remarks used to throw Gladstone into a white fury of rage. "You call it amusing, I call it devilish," was, according to common talk, one of Gladstone's remarks on such an occasion.

I also heard Mill's speech when he moved the Women's Suffrage amendment to the 1867 Reform Bill; its terms were to omit the word " man " from the enfranchising clause and substitute the word " person." The speech was a masterpiece of close reasoning, tinged here and there by deep emotion. It thrilled me to hear my sister and her successful efforts to open the medical profession to women referred to. But perhaps what interested me most of all was the evidently powerful impression the speech made on the House. This was particularly shown in the case of Mr. John Bright. His brother Jacob, and all his sisters with whom I was acquainted, were Suffragists, but they had not succeeded in taking the most distinguished member of their family with them. As soon as Mill rose to speak John Bright entered the House and flung himself into the corner seat below the gangway on the left of the Chair, just below where Mill was speaking. Bright had a mocking smile on his face, which everyone who remembers it will recall had a strong natural capacity in the curve of the mouth, even in repose, for expressing contempt. He crossed his legs and swung the one that was uppermost backwards and forwards. His whole figure suggested a strong mixture of dislike and scorn ; but as Mill developed his arguments this gradually changed. The swinging leg became still, the mocking smile vanished, and when the division was taken Bright's name was actually among the seventy-three who voted for Mill's amendment. Bright, however, soon had a relapse ; he was by nature an Anti-Suffragist, and this was the one and only time that he gave a vote in favour of extending representative institutions to women. Though the amendment had been defeated by more than two to one, we were elated by the success, much greater than we had expected, of Mill's speech, and were especially glad that the division had not been on party lines. Mr. Russell Gurney, Recorder of London, and a much-respected Conservative, acted as teller with Mr. Mill for the Suffragists, and in the division list, if pairs and tellers were added, it was found that the total number of our friends had been eighty, of whom ten were Conservatives. From that time until our final victory in 1918 we were successful in keeping the question of women's franchise on non-party lines. Of course this had drawbacks, but these, such as they were, were greatly outweighed by advantages, especially as our chief work for many years consisted in active Suffrage propaganda in the country ; but the story of this must be left for a later chapter.

Chapter VII

CAMBRIDGE IN THE 'SIXTIES AND 'SEVENTIES

TO ENJOY A SHARE in the social life of Cambridge was an even greater change for me than either London or Salisbury had afforded. My first glimpse of it was in 1867 at the summer meeting of the Fellows of Trinity Hall, my husband's college. It took me some time to apprehend the immense gulf which then separated the Heads of Colleges from persons of inferior University rank. This gulf flowed between the ladies as deep and strong as between members of the more exalted sex. The seats allotted to women in the University Church, Great St. Mary's, were labelled " For the Ladies of Heads of Houses," " For the Ladies of Doctors of Divinity," " For the Ladies of Professors," and so forth ; and socially the laws of precedence were most strictly observed, and controlled with the utmost rigour the movements of the ladies leaving the table after a dinner party as on all other occasions. Thus as the ladies were leaving the dining-room I have seen two approaching the door at the same moment, pause and look at each other, each hesitating, each dreading to take a false step, then A said to B, " Has your husband taken his Doctor's degree ? " B replied, " No, it is to be to-morrow." This settled everything, and A said with decision, " Then *I* go first," and swept out with great dignity. The gulf between University and not University was even more profound. There was a charming old Admiral [1] who, after serving his country on all the oceans of the world, chose Cambridge as his residence when age compelled him to retire. He was entirely ignored in the University, but chancing to meet the Head of a College in some favourite summer resort, the two became quite friendly, took walks and had talks together, and occasionally enjoyed a friendly rubber in the evening ; but the Head explained before they parted that this pleasant intimacy could not be continued in Cambridge. This seems incredible, but it was an actual fact and a characteristic one. The Heads of Colleges considered themselves quite a race apart, and could not demean themselves by social intercourse with anyone below the University rank of a Doctor of Divinity or a Professor. The wife of a Head of a College who was also a Canon of Ely, and therefore in residence there for some months every year, was asked on her return to Cambridge what sort of society she found in Ely. " Very, very quiet," she replied. " Well, it is just what Cambridge would be without the Heads."

In Cambridge, to the rank and file of ordinary M.A.'s, this reply caused great amusement, for the Heads of Houses were not ordinarily regarded as capable of adding materially to the gaiety of nations.

I have one more story on this point. Two ladies, each married to a member of the University, were talking together in Cambridge ; they passed a terrace of attractive-looking houses, and one said to the other, " Those look nice houses ; it is a pity no one lives in them." The other rather less than the first subdued to what she worked in, remarked, " They don't look empty " ; and the first rejoined, " Oh, I mean no one belonging to the University ! "

It is probable that these absurdities were on the wane when I first knew Cambridge in 1867 ; but it is rather

[1] This was Admiral Davies, the father of Augusta Webster, the poetess.

interesting to have seen them in actual existence, a going concern, before they were overwhelmed by the demo-cratic flood of later years. Notwithstanding these little oddities, I very soon came to love and value Cambridge with all my heart. We had most delightful friends there, and our four months every year, from October until opening of Parliament in February, became the happiest of my life.

Among our intimate friends, and the one who more than anyone else with the exception of my husband introduced me to the Cambridge world, was the Rev. H. A. Morgan, Fellow and Tutor, and afterwards Master, of Jesus College. I first made his acquaintance during the summer meetings of the Fellows of Trinity Hall in 1867 just referred to. Mr. Morgan was in residence at this time, and we saw him almost daily. A majority of my husband's Cambridge friends were away, as it was the beginning of the Long Vacation ; but Mr. Morgan introduced them all to me vicariously by his extraordinary gifts of mimicry. He could not only mimic voice and manner, he could also imagine with ludicrous probability what each one of them would say on any given occasion. It was thus I first made the acquaintance of Dr. Kennedy, Professor of Greek, and Canon of Ely, formerly Head Master of Shrews-bury, where Mr. Morgan had been one of his pupils. H. A. M., as he was often called, had endless stories, all affectionate and appreciative, but intensely amusing, of his old master ; he could also cause to live before one the then Master of Jesus College, and Dr. Westmoreland, Dr. Campion, of Queens' College, the Rev. James Porter, of Peterhouse, Dr. Bateson, the Master of St. John's, and many others. All these, when I came to live in Cambridge in the following October, I felt I already knew, not only the sound of their voices, but their main characteristics.

Out of a crowd of amusing memories I select a few descriptive of Dr. Kennedy ; I had made his acquaintance before I had ever seen him, through Mr. Morgan. I knew that he was warm-hearted, irascible, explosive, easily bursting into sudden rages about nothing, and as easily appeased ; also that he was the author of a Latin Grammar which he considered unapproachable in excellence and believed that every one else knew by heart. Therefore, when I met him in the flesh I was not at all surprised that he should say in the course of a rather lengthy dissertation, " But I need not dwell upon this point, for I have expressed myself already in the preface to my Grammar, which, no doubt, you've read."

Let no one suppose that Dr. Kennedy, with his passionate and vehement temperament, was otherwise than very tender-hearted. I have seen the tears coursing down his cheeks as he told of the barbarous cruelty of the criminal law in the days of his youth ; of a poor woman being condemned to death for stealing a loaf of bread to save her children from starving, her husband, the natural breadwinner, having been seized by the Press Gang for the recruiting of the Navy. Once—but this was later, during the Turko-Russian War of 1877—I was next him at a dinner party at Peterhouse, and had been rather exasperated by a continuous flow of well-rounded periods extolling the Turks—as gentlemen, and so forth—and execrating the Russians. Presently, changing his tone a little, he said : " It is an interesting problem to conjecture what would have been the fate of Europe if the Turks had not been driven back from the gates of Vienna by John Sobieski in 1683." I then put in my oar, and said blandly, " I suppose, Dr. Kennedy, you regret that they were driven back." He turned on me in a fury, his little black eyes flashing fire, and said, " Ye dare to say so," and so forth. I just held on, and knew his wrath would die down as quickly as it had awakened. One of Mr. Morgan's favourite stories about Dr. Kennedy related to an old friend, who had actually written a Latin Grammar himself and had had sufficient temerity to send a copy of it to Dr. Kennedy. By return of post came the book back to its writer with this note : " I send you back your Grammar, which you have not hesitated in the depth of your impertinence to send me." But a few posts later came another letter : " Dear So-and-so, I am afraid I wrote you a hasty note yesterday. *The stupid servant posted it ; but it was never intended to be posted.* My daughter Julia generally sees to these things, but unfortunately she was out," etc. The two daughters, Marion and Julia, were among my dearest friends in Cambridge : they were warm supporters of opening University education to women ; they were good scholars themselves : their father had seen to that. Julia, in particular, having made a special study of Anglo-Saxon, acted for many years as tutor in this subject in Newnham College. They extended every possible assistance to the successful founding of Newnham, and, of course, they were keen Suffragists. Their father was in complete sympathy with them over women's education, but was not so sound as to their political aspirations. The daughters, however, had got him on so far that he favoured the admission of unmarried women to the Parliamentary franchise, but thought the foundations of society would be undermined if married women had the right to vote. Meeting my husband and others at a College dinner, Dr. Kennedy expressed this view with his usual emphasis, even going so far as to say that he supposed no one could be so foolish as to advocate the giving the right to vote to married women. My husband here joined in and challenged this opinion, saying that he himself was strongly in favour of married women voting. The result was an immediate explosion from Dr. Kennedy

directed—not against my husband, but against his
daughters. " Then I've been deceived ; my daughter
Julia has deceived me," and so forth.   Julia, of course,
was not there to defend herself : but there is no doubt
that the rest of the battle was fought to a finish in another
place, and that Julia did not succumb.   She was extraordinarily like her father : most thorough in anything
she undertook, explosive, irritable, and lovable.   Something went wrong between herself and the Newnham
Council which caused her official withdrawal from it,
but she remained a lifelong and most valuable friend of
the College, of which her sister was the hon. secretary.
Both sisters were stalwarts in every phase of the emancipation of women, especially in the matter of education.
Dr. Kennedy was one of the earliest and best friends of
the College.   It will be remembered that at first, when
Newnham was in its infancy, it was thought over-
ambitious to give it the name " College " ; therefore, in
its earlier years and when there was only one Hall, it
was called Newnham Hall.   As years passed and the
success of Newnham became more generally recognized,
and the number of students desiring entrance increased,
another Hall was added and a new name was adopted.
Dr. Kennedy, who was then on the Council of Newnham,
was one day returning from one of its meetings and
met at the ferry boat, which then conveyed pedestrians
across the Cam at Coe Fen, a friend of ours, Mr. Beck,
of Trinity Hall, who was going in the opposite direction.
Mr. Beck, of course, knew Dr. Kennedy by sight and
by reputation (everyone in Cambridge did), but had
never been introduced to him.   As soon as they were
within speaking distance, Dr. Kennedy, very full of the
subject which had occupied his morning, burst out in
triumph, " We've made it a college ! "

As I am writing now of the early days of Newnham, I
cannot forbear mentioning what I have always regarded

as an honour, viz. that Professor Henry Sidgwick, the real founder of Newnham, asked me and my husband to lend our drawing-room for the first meeting ever held in Cambridge in its support. So far as I can remember, this must have been in 1870. We were then occupying a furnished house which possessed a drawing-room of suitable size for such an occasion. I therefore recognize that the birth of Newnham under my roof was more or less accidental ; nevertheless, such is human folly, I go on being proud and pleased about it. I know that Philippa was a little baby girl at the time, but was old enough to be brought in at the tea-drinking stage at the end of the proceedings and to toddle about in her white frock and blue sash among the guests. I thought in 1890 that no one but myself remembered this, but when Professor Sidgwick wrote to congratulate me on my daughter's place in the mathematical tripos of that year, he said, " Who would have thought, at that first meeting at your house, that the little girl who was trotting about would one day be above the Senior Wrangler ? " I will add one more anecdote of Professor Sidgwick because it is characteristic of him. Early each autumn, when my husband and I were preparing to transfer ourselves to Cambridge, one of our pieces of work was to select the books we needed to take with us. My view was that with access to the University Library and other libraries we did not need to carry many books with us : moreover, had we not Dr. Ferrers, of unbounded friendliness and stupendous and accurate memory, next door ? It was our London bookshelves which needed nourishing and cherishing rather than those at Cambridge. So I got into the habit of weeding out from London the books that must be housed somewhere, but were dead heads, volumes that never had been read and never would be read. As years passed on there were a good many of this type on our Cambridge shelves. It happened that Dr. and Mrs. Sidgwick occupied our house at Cambridge for several months after their marriage. When we all met again at the beginning of the October term I happened to mention in Dr. Sidgwick's presence that our Cambridge books, those which stayed there always, were mainly those that never had been read and never would be read by anyone. Everyone knows that he stammered, but stammered with great skill, adding thereby to the point and effectiveness of his remarks. He at once said, " I d-did rather wonder what your p-principle of selection had been."

Another of our very great friends at Cambridge was James Stuart, of Trinity, the creator of the University extension movement. He was a Scot, and had come on to Cambridge with a brilliant reputation from his first University, St. Andrews. He was one of the wittiest and most delightful of men, equally great in things grave as in things gay. He would keep us laughing by the hour together with stories of his youth in Scotland.

He was one of those men who have a strong attraction for children. Philippa, usually a shy child, was not shy with him. She christened him " the cassawary," in connection with the well-known rhyme which he had taught her. Towards the end of his life he wrote his reminiscences, and when I read them I seem to hear his very voice telling us his Scotch stories. One, which I do not think appears in the book, referred to some of the difficulties of a Scot in England. When he became the first Professor of Mechanics and Engineering he had the happy thought of bringing with him to Cambridge from his native Fife a working engineer who knew as much of the practical side of the job as Stuart did of the scientific side. He established this good man in a workman's family in Cambridge ; and for a little time all went well. It was the period when all

England was agog about Turkish atrocities in Bulgaria. Disraeli had referred to them in the House as mere rumour, " coffee-house babble," but this only added to the excited indignation they aroused, especially when details of the cruelties were published in the Liberal Press, authenticated by the signatures of well-known special correspondents. It was during this excitement that the Scottish mechanic had become a member of an English working-man's household. One day Professor Stuart was called away from his work to see the head of this family, who told him at once that other arrangements must be made for the lodging of the Scottish engineer. " My wife is terrified of him, sir, and can't get any rest or peace as long as he's in our house." Professor Stuart, greatly surprised, for he knew the Scot well, and was sure he was a most decent fellow, asked for details. " Well, sir, only yesterday in the evening I was out and Mackenzie, he was sitting over the fire, and he presently jumps up and says to my wife, ' *Will I rake out y'r ribs ?* ' and she can't stand it no longer." James Stuart was far too good a diplomatist to laugh, but he assured his visitor most seriously that the words quoted were entirely harmless, and if rendered into English meant nothing more than " Shall I poke the fire ? " Henceforth all was peace, and the Scot was welcomed as a house-mate.

Professor Stuart was frequently one of our riding companions. The wide strips of grass at the side of nearly all the Cambridgeshire roads made it a delightful riding country, and we not infrequently got as far as Newmarket and had a gallop on the heath. Our more horsey friends used to say that no one who was not a professor of mechanics and engineering could have stuck in the saddle with such a seat on a horse as Stuart had : he enjoyed this joke as much as any of us. With all his wit and keen enjoyment of life there was a deeply serious side to his nature. He was an active fellow-labourer with Josephine Butler in her crusade against the C.D. Acts : he had meetings for young men in his rooms on the subject, and worked earnestly for the establishment (still far from being realized) of an equal moral standard for men and women. I remember Mr. E. A. Beck, of Trinity Hall (in later years its Master), saying to us, " I don't know Stuart, I wish I did, but I know that when Middlemore comes back from seeing him he looks as if he had taken the sacrament."

He was a strong moral influence, an active antiseptic. Every society of which Stuart was a member was purer and stronger for his presence in it. After my husband's death Stuart succeeded him as Member for Hackney ; but somehow he was not the success as a politician that he had been in Cambridge. I think he got caught up in the toils of party, and was too much dominated by his personal loyalty and devotion to his leader, W. E. Gladstone. There are, however, many interesting letters of his in a volume arranged by Mrs. Drew and published by Nisbet & Co. about 1911, called *Some Hawarden Letters*, which show how he was working still, in that arid soil, to get some recognition of the injury done to the whole of society in giving no political representation to women and by the mass of law and custom which differentiates unjustly between the sexes. He married Miss Laura Colman, daughter of his friend Mr. J. J. Colman, Member for Norwich. Mr. Colman was the head of a large business in Norwich, and, noting James Stuart's organizing capacities, he rather rapidly transferred the management of the concern to his son-in-law. Residents in Norwich at that time have told me how this was generally considered in the business world there a more than doubtful experiment. A University Professor suddenly put at the head of a large firm ! ! !

One can imagine how the step awakened something akin to consternation. The croakers speedily found out they were wrong, and confessed that the firm under Stuart's direction was better managed than it had ever been before.

There are many other Cambridge friends I should like to write about. There were Professor and Mrs. Cowell ; he was the cousin of my brother-in-law, Herbert Cowell, and, as all the world knows, a most distinguished Oriental scholar. If it had not been for his wife he probably would have wasted his genius for Oriental learning : but she insisted on his freeing himself from the ties which bound him to Ipswich and induced him to follow his real bent, first as student at Oxford, and later as Professor in the University of Calcutta. He was devoted to children, and liked nothing better than to entertain them with Eastern fairy stories. She was the sister of Maria Charlesworth, author of *Ministering Children*, but did not care to be thus described. " If I had wished it," she used to say, " I think I could have written quite as well as dear Maria." But she did not wish it. Her great work was the fostering of her husband's genius. The Cowells were intimate friends of Edward Fitzgerald. Gossip said that " Fitz " had even contemplated making an offer of marriage to Miss Charlesworth, but put off and put off and put off taking any definite step in this direction, when Professor Cowell stepped in and made it for ever impossible. Fitzgerald, as everyone knows, is one of our Suffolk worthies, and was a great lover of Aldeburgh and of its seamen. He was visiting Aldeburgh in 1882 when my husband, accompanied by Philippa, visited him. He instantly asked her what she was reading, and what stories she liked best. She replied, " Thackeray's and George Eliot's." He exclaimed in horror, " What can your mother be thinking of to let you read such books ? "

He gave her, perhaps as an antidote, a *Life of George Crabbe*, written by the poet's son, and also a selection made by himself of Crabbe's poems. I am afraid both of these books were added to the collection in our Cambridge house.

Another of our intimate friends in Cambridge was J. F. Moulton, afterwards Lord Moulton, the brilliant Senior Wrangler of 1868, who afterwards made a name for himself in science and law, and rendered extraordinarily effective service to his country during the war years 1914–18. Details of this should be read in the interesting biography written in 1922 by his son. Then there were the Peiles, whom we first knew in their charming house at Trumpington. He afterwards became the Master of Christ's College. They also were among the founders of Newnham, and one of the Halls is suitably called by their name. Mrs. Peile was a cousin of Lord Kitchener, and he was their guest in the Master's Lodge at Christ's when he came up for an honorary degree after his campaign in the Soudan. He was infuriated by the disorderly rowdiness of the undergraduates, and roared at them that he wished he had them in the Soudan. This they interpreted as a compliment, but General Kitchener did not mean it as such : he meant that if they had been " Tommies " he would have taught them how to behave.

One of our very dear friends in Cambridge was Miss Jane McLeod Smith. She had been among the earliest of the Newnham students, before any formal recognition had been given to them by the University. She had a little day school in Cambridge for boys and girls, children of her friends. Besides Philippa, she had as pupils Hugh Ferrers, Hester Peile, Willie Moulton, and several others. Her strong point as an educationist was her love of great literature, which she was successful in passing on to her pupils. The one I know best can instantly tell you where almost any passage from Shakespeare occurs, and if she goes to see a play can say at once which lines have been left out, besides knowing by heart, and therefore possessing for life, the greatest poems by Milton, Shelley, etc.

The little school was managed on original lines : prizes occupied a very subordinate place in it. However, there was a Latin prize at Christmas one year ; this was awarded to Hester Peile. On returning home Willie Moulton was asked by his father, Dr. Moulton (brother of our friend J. F. M., the Head Master of the Leys School, and one of the learned revisers of the Old Testament), who had taken the Latin prize : on being told, he said in a reproving tone, " I am surprised, Willie, that you should have allowed the Latin prize to be won by a girl," whereupon Willie rejoined, " Well, papa, you see Hester has such a clever father." We were all very pleased by this counter-check courteous, and thought it was a sign that Willie Moulton shared in the readiness and mental gifts of his family.

It is tempting to go on piling up anecdotes of our Cambridge friends, but if I let myself go my story would be too long for my readers' patience. The very names reawaken in my mind so many memories. There were Dr. and Mrs. Bateson, and a family of very attractive children, several of whom were destined to become my lifelong friends. Dr. Bateson was Master of St. John's and the leader of the University Liberals : Mrs. Bateson was a very keen supporter of the Women's Movement in all its branches ; I used to call her " my best woman " and James Stuart my " best man " among our Cambridge friends. Then there were Professor and Mrs. Miller, and their three daughters ; Emma, the second, became my fast friend. She helped me when I was reading Dante, as she was far more proficient than I in Italian and had, moreover, the scholar's mind and exactitude. Mrs. Miller was a real wit : her sayings went all over Cambridge ; though I often thought the more stodgy members of the University did not appreciate them as highly as they deserved. She was an artist, too. Her etchings had been shown to Ruskin, who had given them his blessing. One of her sayings I am tempted to quote. It has Mrs. Miller's special quality of the unexpected : " Oh ! how glad I am Newnham and Girton didn't exist in my time ! " she said to me. I exclaimed, as I was sure she meant I should, " Why, Mrs. Miller ? " She rejoined at once, " Because I know my husband would have married one of them and not me." I have already referred to Dr. and Mrs. Ferrers, our next-door neighbours in Brookside, and the kindest of kind friends. Their eldest child, Gilbert, was the most extraordinarily gifted boy I have ever known : he was as wonderful (so I was informed) in his special line, mathematics, as the infant Mozart had been in music. His early death nearly killed his parents, and I was in my degree pierced to the heart by it more than by any other death which had touched me closely since I lost my dear sister Louie in 1867.

In looking over these notes I should like to mention that one of the great pleasures of our Cambridge life was the amount of good music we were able to hear, not only the first-rate musical services at King's and Trinity, but chamber music in our own home or in the rooms of our friends. One of our very kindest music makers was Mr. Sedley Taylor. He was a musical enthusiast for all sorts of music. His voice was not his strong point : but he had the born musician's gift, without exactly singing, of being able to present the very soul of a song, whether it were " Father O'Flynn " or " Adelaide." He was devoted to my husband, and was always ready to come to play to him whatever he liked best. Then we also had the advantage of hearing

Mr. (afterwards Sir) Charles Villiers Stanford, who rapidly became the leader of the musical life of Cambridge. I remember particularly hearing him with delight in Mr. J. F. Moulton's rooms at Christ's. It was fitting in Milton's college that the " Blest pair of sirens voice and verse" should wed their divine sounds there.

We had some very charming neighbours living about ten miles from Cambridge in Mr. and Mrs. W. H. Hall, of Six-Mile Bottom. Mrs. Hall was French, and Mr. Hall in his youth had fought, as a volunteer, in Garibaldi's army. They had a wide circle of foreign friends ; many of them were of great distinction. They once brought Tourguéniev over to us to luncheon, and he allowed us to talk to him about his books, especially about *Virgin Soil*, which we had just read and admired very much. I took him round to see Newnham, and introduced him to Miss Jane Harrison, whom we found in her room deep in Plato.

I remember Tourguéniev saying to me as we came away : " What would I not give to see colleges for women like this in my own country ! "

But there are still two names knocking at the gate of my memory : those of Dr. and Mrs. Geldart, the Master of Trinity Hall, and his wife. A volume in the style of *Cranford* would be needed to do them justice ; they belonged so entirely to a past generation —almost to the eighteenth century. Dr. Geldart had acquired his considerable fortune in a romantic way. Having secured the best, that is the middle, seat on the outside of a stage-coach for a night journey, he found when he took possession of it that his neighbour, a man much older than himself, had the less desirable place, where, if the coach lurched or if the passenger dropped asleep, he was not unlikely to be pitched off. With characteristic courtesy the younger man offered the elder the more desirable seat. This led to friendly conversation, and at the end of the journey the two exchanged cards. One of the travellers was named Geldart and the other Gildart. This led to further friendly talk, and the older man asked the younger to visit him : their friendship ripened, and eventually Gildart and Geldart were merged in one, Geldart leaving his fortune to Gildart on condition of his assuming the former's name.

The younger fellows of Trinity Hall used to say that they were spending their lives convoying old ladies across Regent Circus, or performing other deeds of desperate daring on behalf of strangers, but no one had ever left them a fortune. The Master of Trinity Hall was a devoted fisherman, and he became in time a great judge of wine and of food. When he ventured into the sphere of theology he was commonly believed to have said that to him the strongest evidence of design in the work of creation was that when salmon went out turbot came in.

The Rev. Henry Latham was the senior tutor at Trinity Hall when I first knew anything about the College. The Master was not infrequently heard to say, " I never have had any opinion of Latham . . . as a judge of wine." He left directions in his will that if he died in term-time the young men (as he called the undergraduates) who attended his funeral were not to have the College sherry—" I never have thought well of the College sherry," said the Master with great solemnity—but they were to have a very good brown sherry from his own cellars. Once, having the honour of sitting next him at a dinner party at his own house, and seeing the array of, I think, four wine-glasses allotted to each plate, he said, very gravely, " No doubt you have wondered, Mrs. Fawcett, that I am not offering my friends hock : I need hardly say how gladly I would have done so : I have some really fine hock ; but," glancing round the large table, " I think there is no one here except myself and your Professor who could fully appreciate it."

Mrs. Geldart was hardly less unique. Her loyalty, for example, to the Royal Family seemed to belong to the time of le Roi Soleil : but all the same she did sometimes venture to criticize. For instance, she was shattered and temporarily estranged by the marriage of Princess Louise to the Marquis of Lorne. She did not recover from the shock for quite a long time. Trinity Hall had a custom of tremendous feastings between Christmas and the New Year. Perhaps this originated at a time when fellows and scholars had less then enough on ordinary occasions. A huge dinner at five o'clock would be followed by a huge supper at ten, day after day for several days. These festivals were appropriately and picturesquely entered in the College accounts as " Christmas exceedings." The Master and Mrs. Geldart superintended the preparations with careful solicitude. The menus were always sent in to them for criticism and approval. A year or two after the Royal marriage just referred to a forgetful steward or cook had placed among the names of half a dozen soups " Potage Princess Louise " : an agitated summons was sent by Mrs. Geldart to the responsible official to come at once on a matter of urgency : he found the good lady literally dancing about in her drawing-room and waving the objectionable menu in her hand. " What does this mean ? " she asked (she lisped a little, especially when excited). " Potage Windsor, all very right and proper ; Potage à la reine, not a word to say against it ; but Potage Princess Louise, *I will not have it :* I never have approved of that marriage." She was strongly opposed to Women's Suffrage ; but she herself had a very grave concern about the orthodoxy of several of the bishops. What good advice she could have given the Prime Minister ! But she had never been approached about these appointments. People like that are not made now, and even fifty or sixty years ago they were extremely rare. Let us not forget to be thankful for having had even a glimpse of them.

Chapter VIII

POLITICS AND MY BEGINNING OF SUFFRAGE WORK

I HAVE NO INTENTION of trying to write my husband's political life, nor to give more than a passing glance at the value of his influence and example in putting new heart and courage into those who were called upon to bear the burden of blindness.

Both of these most worthy tasks have been done, and done by master hands : the political life of my husband by his friend Leslie Stephen (*Life of Henry Fawcett*, published by Smith, Elder & Co.), and the story of what his example had done for the blind, by Miss Winifred Holt, now Mrs. Holt Mather, an American lady who has devoted her life to helping the blind to lead lives of active usefulness. Her book, *A Beacon for the Blind* (Constable & Co.), was written just before the war : it was the result of many months' work, devoted by the author while she was in England to getting into touch with as many as possible of my husband's personal friends. Her book is thus a personal record full of vivid picturesque touches, and has, I know, been the means of lifting up many blind men and women from apathy and despair to lives of active usefulness, and therefore happiness.

From the early years of our marriage, my husband was constantly urging me to write. Without his perpetual encouragement I certainly should not have embarked on authorship at the age of twenty-one. I was also helped and encouraged by his old friend Mr. Alexander Macmillan, the head of the publishing firm which bears his name. My first article appeared in 1868, in *Macmillan's Magazine*. Its subject was " The Lectures for Women in Cambridge," which had lately been started by Henry Sidgwick. These lectures proved to be the seed of which, in a few years, Newnham College was the fruit. I mention this little article partly because I received £7 for it. It was the first money I had ever earned. So I made a sort of Feast of the First Fruits, and gave my £7 to the fund then being formed for paying Mr. Mill's expenses at the General Election of that year. It was about this time that I began to have business talks with Mr. Macmillan. There were many amusing contrasts between him and my husband. On one occasion, after a great talk on all things in heaven and earth, Mr. Macmillan, who had the Scot's turn for metaphysics and philosophy as well as the Scot's eye for the main chance, exclaimed, " I often ask myself, Why am I here ? " Whereupon my husband at once rejoined, " Why to publish Barnard Smith's arithmetic, of course." This friendly chaff Mr. Macmillan took in very good part. He was a real friend to both of us. A recent writer who pretends to describe a violent personal altercation between my husband and his publisher is entirely wrong : there was never anything between them but mutual respect and hearty good will. Mr. Macmillan's business experience convinced him that there was a demand for an elementary book upon Political Economy, on the same lines as my husband's manual and of J. S. Mill's important work. He was convinced I could write this book, and my husband was of the same opinion. Mr. Macmillan gave me sound practical advice about such matters as the headings of the paragraphs, in leaded type to draw attention to a new subject, and so on. The little puzzles and the questions at the end of each chapter were a later thought and did not appear until the second edition. They were recommended to me by Mr. E. E. Bowen, of Harrow, and were based upon his practical experience of teaching a class.

From this time onwards until his death in 1896 Mr. Macmillan was among my most valued friends. My little book passed through many editions. It is now in its tenth, and is still in some demand. Writing came more easily to me than public speaking ever did, although for many years work for Women's Suffrage compelled me to do so much of it. When our victory for Women's Suffrage was celebrated in 1918, I had been in the collar as a speaker on its behalf for fifty years, and I own that one of my first thoughts was, " Then I shall never have to make another Suffrage speech ! " I could not have kept it up as long as I did if it had not been for the constant fuel my flames received from the Anti-Suffragists, and especially from the quite priceless *Anti-Suffrage Review*.

It was Mrs. Peter Taylor who first gave me a place among the active workers for Suffrage. I joined her Committee immediately after my marriage. She presided at the first public meeting in London in its advocacy, and I was one of the speakers : a humble one, of course, for among the others were J. S. Mill and my husband. Among my books, one of my most cherished possessions is a copy of Mill's *Subjection of Women* (original edition) given to me by the author. I was terrified by the ordeal of my first speech, but scraped through somehow. A few days later a then well-known member of Parliament, Mr. C. R., referred publicly in the House to the appearance of Mrs. Taylor and myself upon a platform to advocate votes for women, as " two ladies, wives of members of this House, who had disgraced themselves,'" and added that he " would not further disgrace them by mentioning their names."

It so happened that a very short time after this my husband and I were spending the week-end in Cambridge, and that most hospitable of men, Mr. James Porter, of Peterhouse, asked us to dine with him. What was my amusement to see Mr. C. R. also among the guests : this amusement was intensified into positive glee when he was asked to take me in to dinner. I could not resist expressing condolences with him on his unfortunate position. Should I ask Mr. Porter to let him exchange me for some other lady who had not disgraced herself ? But after we had let off steam a little in this way, I found him quite an agreeable neighbour at the table, and so far as I knew he never again publicly held up any woman to contempt for advocating the enfranchisement of her sex. After all, what he had said was very mild compared to Horace Walpole's abuse of Mary Wollstonecraft as " a hyena in petticoats."

My first speech of any length in support of Women's Suffrage was made in Brighton, my husband's constituency, in 1870. Several members of his Election Committee were aghast at the proposal, and thought I should injure his prospects of re-election. But we had three great friends, political and personal, in the town— Mr. Willett, Mr. Carpenter, and Mr. Merrifield ; none of these discouraged me. Mr. Willett was a wealthy man, a brewer, full of active benevolence, and a great collector of all kinds of beautiful things : china, silver, pictures, old furniture, etc. I think his house is the only one in which I have ever enjoyed the privilege of having a Memling in my bedroom. He did not exactly smile on my proposal to address a Brighton meeting in support of women's votes, but neither did he exactly frown. He had once been a determined opponent of the Rev. F. W. Robertson when he knew little or nothing about him : later, he had become his ardent admirer, but it was then too late, for the great preacher was dead ; it was a lifelong regret to Mr. Willett, of which he frequently spoke, that, living as he had done for years in the same town as Robertson, he had never heard him preach. This memory possibly softened his instinctive opposition to what I was then proposing. Mr. Carpenter was a delightful old gentleman with a charming family of musical sons and daughters. He had formerly been in the Navy. His son, Edward Carpenter, so well known now as a writer on socialist and revolutionary lines, was then a junior Fellow of my husband's college, and had taken Orders. He was for a short time in charge of the Trinity Hall Church, St. Edwards. When he became a poet and one of the earliest of English appreciators of Walt Whitman, and also an ardent opponent of modern developments of civilization, he sent me his little book *Towards Democracy* : my copy was characteristically bound into its cover upside down. On looking back at these far-away days and our friendship with the Carpenter family, it will be easily realized how pleased I was, in April 1918, to learn that the Captain Alfred Carpenter, of the *Vindictive*, who took such a distinguished part in the organization and leadership of the successful attack on the Zeebrugge mole, was the grandson of my old friend at Brighton.

Of the other family in Brighton who were our warm friends, I could until the other day write in the present tense. But I can do so no longer ; my dear old friend died very suddenly in May 1924. Mr. Merrifield was a barrister with none of the faults generally attributed to members of his profession. He was one of the very best men I have ever known : upright, just, and full of moral enthusiasm. His profession had taught him careful accuracy and caution in forming a judgment, but had never dimmed his idealism, nor his constant seeking after better things than up to that time had been possible. He welcomed every reasonable proposal for improving the status of women, advocating their education, the repeal of the barbaric laws which subordinated their individuality to father, husband or son, and consequently was a born Suffragist. His wife was half French. Her father, M. de Gaudrion, had been chosen in his youth to be one of the pages of Marie Antoinette, but before his commission had been confirmed, though not before his trousseau, including muff and earrings, had been provided, he caught small-pox and lost the good looks which were as essential to his position at Court as his quarterings. When the storm of the Revolution broke M. de Gaudrion remained faithful to the Royalist cause : he joined the army of the Princes ; and, returning to France after the Restoration, he was placed in command of the French troops at St. Malo, where he met his future (English) wife and where Mrs. Merrifield was born.

The French strain was very obvious and very attractive in Mrs. Merrifield, and in her children. To France our friend Mr. Merrifield gave a passion of loyalty as great almost as that which he felt for his own country. His intense anxiety during the earlier years of the war of 1914–18 almost broke down his health, and he rendered notable service to the Allied Cause by his letters to the Press, and other writings in which he set forth with masterly clarity the strength and the justice of their cause, specially emphasizing the French point of view. When the final victory came in 1918 it brought to him something that was almost a renewal of his youth. He was then over ninety, and something of an invalid ; but he was an athletic invalid, for his bathchair could be seen dashing over the Downs round Brighton at a pace and for distances that were simply amazing. Well,

he was my best friend in Brighton over my project to
give a suffrage address there in 1870. I feel very proud
of my three chief friends in Brighton, and proudest of
all of Mr. Merrifield. The meeting at Brighton just
referred to was held on the 23rd March 1870. The
chair was taken by Mr. Carpenter, who was President
of the local Liberal Association. Mr. and Mrs.
Merrifield, were on the platform, and so were their two
daughters, then little girls. Mr. Hack and Mr. Marriage
Wallis, well-known and much-respected Quakers in the
town, were also present, and my husband, of course.
Everybody was very kind about the meeting. A
working man in the audience proposed to start a petition
to Parliament there and then in the room in favour of
the enfranchisement of women ; but the Chairman
ruled this out of order. Nothing is duller reading than
speeches on issues which are dead and gone, and I have
no intention of giving any account of my oration in
What I Remember. In fact, I do not remember it at
all, but I know that it was printed as a pamphlet, and
I hope was not without its uses as Suffrage propaganda.
Our friend Walter Morrison, then M.P. for Plymouth,
told me that he read it all through on one of his railway
journeys down to his constituency, and reproduced a
good deal of it when he was addressing a meeting there.
It is a pleasure to reflect that Suffrage seed sown there
in 1870 may possibly have had some share in preparing
the soil for the return of Lady Astor as the first woman
M.P. in 1919.

My husband meanwhile was working hard at his own
subjects : our relations with India, and the unfair
burdens thrown on her finances ; the prevention of
enclosures and the preservation of open spaces ; University Reform and the removal of religious disabilities.
When I first knew Cambridge no honest Jew could
take a degree, for it would have necessitated swearing

a solemn oath, in the presence of the Vice-Chancellor, " on the true faith of a Christian." This outrageous exclusiveness was not completely broken down until 1877, and the final blow was dealt by Parliament : it was not a reform pushed through by the governing body of the University itself. The heat and bitterness engendered by the compulsory abolition of religious tests in the older universities can best be measured by looking back for a moment at some of the controversial writings of the time. Dean Burgon, for instance, spoke of the abolition of tests as characterized by " inherent and essential deformity," " its aim, its successful aim," he continued, having been " the disestablishment of Christianity in the Colleges." [1]

Part of my husband's gradual alienation from Mr. Gladstone arose from what he considered the great man's weakness on the subject of religious freedom. One of his sayings about Mr. Gladstone was that " he would go as far as he dared on the road to economic and fiscal reform, but only as far as he was forced on the road to religious freedom." This divergence between the two men was intensified by Gladstone's attempt to carry a Bill for creating a new University in Ireland which was to consist of an amalgamation of all the existing Colleges of University standing. These were severally representative of the religious differences which had always caused such deep divergence in Irish life ; the difficulty arising from bringing together these heterogeneous elements into a single University was to be met in Gladstone's Bill by excluding from the University curriculum theology, moral philosophy, and modern history. My husband attacked these proposals with all his strength. What right had any educational institution, he urged, to be called a University in which history,

[1] See Sermon preached before the University of Oxford on Trinity Sunday, 8th June 1884.

theology, and philosophy were forbidden to be taught? In his view, this was almost a sin against the Holy Ghost. On practical grounds, too, the scheme was futile, for it satisfied none of the contending parties in Ireland. In spite of the great Liberal majority which had been returned in 1868, Mr. Gladstone's University Bill was defeated by 287 to 284 in 1873, and the Government received a staggering blow. My husband's University Bill, removing the last traces of religious exclusiveness from the Constitution of Trinity College, Dublin, was then accepted by the Government and passed into law. I do not think Mr. Gladstone ever forgave my husband for this defeat of his own measure and the passing into law of its rival. Mr. Gladstone did not easily brook opposition, especially successful opposition, and my husband, for his part, never needed Mr. R. Kipling's advice to the students of St. Andrews in 1923, and was always ready to say, " At any price I can pay I will own myself."

Chapter IX

VISITS TO IRELAND

ONE OF THE IMMEDIATE RESULTS of these events in our own personal life was a visit to Dublin and other parts of Ireland in order to enable my husband to have consultations with Dr. Lloyd, the Provost of Trinity College, Dublin, and other University authorities. It was our first visit to Ireland, but I went there repeatedly in later years, visiting friends in connection with Suffrage work. On our first visit we stayed in lodgings in Dublin for about a fortnight, and met many most interesting people, among them Dr. Lloyd, Dr. Ingram, Mrs. Rowan Hamilton, and Sir Robert Kane, a man of science and Commissioner of Irish Education. We mingled for a time in a most delightful society, and I think I never in any other place had seen, in social gatherings, so much beauty and such distinguished and charming men and women. In our lodgings we had a very clever and nimble-minded little maid. When the last day of our visit approached and we were occupied in preparing for our departure, we told her that we were too busy to receive visitors. But presently we heard our bell, and the little girl ran into our room with important intelligence on every feature. " It's Sir Robert Kane," she said. " I know y'said y'didn't want to see anybody ; but I know you and the master like him, so I told him I wasn't quite certain whether y'were in or whether y'were out. Now are

94

y'in or are y'out?" This was so clever and so Irish that we never forgot it.

Before returning to England we paid a visit in the south-west to Mr. Townshend Trench, Lord Lansdowne's agent in Kerry. Mr. Trench's house was in a very lovely situation with the broad Kenmare River, almost an arm of the sea, in one direction, and the Kerry mountains in the other. I think we owed this very attractive invitation from Mr. Trench to Lord Edmond Fitzmaurice, Lord Lansdowne's brother, who was an intimate friend of ours. We had a most interesting visit, Mr. Trench keeping up a continuous stream of Irish stories, inimitably told, which we both thoroughly enjoyed. Before our visit came to an end Mr. Trench turned on me and said he knew I hadn't believed one word he had said since I had been there. It hadn't occurred to me either to believe or disbelieve his anecdotes. They were among the things that were good in themselves, whether true or untrue.

Mr. Trench gave us the opportunity of seeing some of the Irish social customs, and very different they were from anything with which we were familiar at home. When the eldest son of a tenant on the estate was of an age to marry and had selected a bride, the farm was transferred from the father to the son, who then had to make a settlement in favour of his parents. But this transaction necessitated a most tremendous amount of bargaining, because the son about to become the tenant had to settle upon his parents, perhaps a cow and four pigs, with enough land for their feed, in order to enable the dispossessed tenant and his wife to live. It was this settlement by the son upon his father which caused such vehement and prolonged conversation. The vehemence and the length were all the more pronounced because the bride-to-be and her parents were also present and took an active part in the proceedings. What appeared an ample and handsome settlement to the one side was resented as miserable parsimony on the other. We were invited to be present at one of these marriage settlement discussions. It was the most curious thing I had ever heard. We were, of course, merely silent auditors, but Mr. Trench took a part, generally, so far as we could judge, a friendly and fair-minded part, tending towards a peaceful solution of the tremendous difficulties involved. In these discussions the mother of the bride was referred to as " the supposed mother-in-law," for, of course, the marriage did not take place till these business affairs had been settled. Coming away, Mr. Trench told us that he was frequently consulted by young men on the Lansdowne estate when they were contemplating marriage as to the direction in which they should allow their affections to flow ; for instance, a young fellow would come to tell Mr. Trench that he had practically a choice between two girls, one had a cow and two pigs ; on the other hand, the one he liked best had a cow and one pig ; and he sought Mr. Trench's advice upon the final casting of the die. Mr. Trench did not hesitate for a moment, but said, " Why marry the girl with the cow and two pigs ? There's not the difference of a pig between any two women in the world." I have since seen this story in various forms, but I think Mr. Trench was entitled to claim it as his own.

The office on the Lansdowne property was in a little building standing apart from any other and some way from the house. It might once have been a lodge. In a conspicuous position on one of the desks was a huge piece of silver plate which had been presented by former tenants on some occasion such as the coming of age or the marriage of an heir to the title and property. When Mr. Trench left the office with us in his company he just turned the key in the lock and dropped it in his pocket. I asked him if it was safe to leave the big piece of presentation silver there where it could be so easily stolen. " Perfectly safe," he said ; " why, what can anyone want with it ? " This seemed to me a very obvious and a very delightful reply to my inquiry, but it was a great testimony to the honesty of the people.

When at Kenmare I heard many terrible stories of the Irish famine. The shopkeepers, when they took down their shutters in the morning, very frequently found dead bodies lying in the street, " mountainy " folk who had held out against starvation so long that they only had strength enough to stagger down the mountain-side into the main street of Kenmare and die there. It was anguish to think of what they must have suffered, and I wondered more than ever at the hundred-weight or so of silver lying quite safe in the unprotected office. It is true, as economists point out, that no one can eat silver or gold, but they do enable the possessor to get food in most cases.

I made many subsequent visits to Ireland, where I formed warm friendships. On one occasion my route led me from Tralee to Limerick, where the trade once flourishing on the splendid river had wasted to nothing. I also visited County Clare, then the centre of a very violent land agitation.

When I was in Tralee driving up the long straggling street I observed that almost every house was licensed to sell spirits, and I was told that magistrates for the most part never refused an application for a spirit licence : they were terrorized into granting it, no matter how great the number already in existence. I heard a good deal of the ill-effects of this system, through which the owner of every draper's, grocer's, or shoemaker's shop was licensed to sell spirits, because women, making the most necessary household purchases, were constantly tempted to drink before a bargain was clinched. On another occasion I was driven about for a whole day by

Mr. Sam Hussey, a well-known land-agent and as witty a man as could be found even in Ireland. Our whole expedition seemed to be for the purpose of showing me the *terrain* of innumerable crimes. Gruesome, my readers may be thinking ; not at all, every stricken field was enlivened by Mr. Sam Hussey's jokes. " This is where the man stood that was shot, and that is where the man stood that shot 'um," said Mr. Hussey. And I, like little Wilhelmine in Southey's verses, was asking, " Why did they do it ? What was it all about ? Was it agrarian ? " and Mr. Hussey replied, " No, no, nothing agrarian at all, merely a friendly affair."

Much later I was in the north of Ireland escorted by my old friend Miss Dorothea Roberts. She was herself an Irishwoman and an eager promoter of many kind schemes for benefiting the girls and women of Donegal and other parts of N.W. Ulster. She had started a knitting industry in which the workers were paid the full value of what they produced, and were thus protected against the exploiter and profiteer. I was struck by the very flourishing look of the village shops in the north, well stocked with excellent grocery of all kinds, tea at 5s. per lb. and so on. But here, too, the trail of crime and compulsion was plainly visible. Boycotting had lately been invented ; it was a form of bitter compulsion on people in humble positions, but caused comparatively little inconvenience to the well-to-do. These could provide themselves with necessaries by parcel post, and I remember very well how one large family enjoyed the joke of seeing the postman labouring up their drive heavily laden, he being the very man who had promoted the boycott against them. But it was very different with people who had only a narrow income to meet necessary expenditure. We stayed the night in a little fishing lodge at G., in County Donegal. The man fulfilled his engagement to look after his employer's fishing—this was what he was paid for ; he was also a Protestant.   These were his only crimes, but he had been severely boycotted, at the time of our visit, for eight months.   His wife told us, with tears in her eyes, that when it was absolutely necessary to go to a shop for tea, sugar, and other things which they could not make for themselves, her husband went at the peril of his life. There was a bridge which it was necessary to cross, and there he was often waylaid by a crowd of rough youths and assailed with sticks and stones.   On the mantelpiece of the bedroom in which I slept there was a small card about two inches long, the size of a gentleman's visiting card, on which were printed, in small type, these words :

> Put thou thy trust in the Lord and be doing good :
> Dwell in the land and verily thou shalt be fed.

I have never forgotten this, and the contrast it presented with the flaming texts with illuminated letters three inches high with which some pious people decorate their rooms.   The date of this was May 1889.   I know that those simple words " verily thou shalt be fed " upheld the heart and courage of these persecuted people.

Another thing which I noticed in the north, as well as in other parts of Ireland, was the extraordinary squalor in which the mass of the people lived.   There was no attempt at beautifying or decorating their homes ; none of the dainty prettiness, neatness, and exquisite cleanliness which make cottage interiors in England so charming.   If we saw even so small an attempt at decoration as was manifested by a scarlet geranium in the window, we unconsciously acquired the habit of astonishment, and would ask, " Who lives there, where the flower is ? "   The answer was generally that it was a family from England or Scotland.   I inquired of those who knew Ireland well if they could account for this difference between the two countries, but never got any satisfactory answer. That it is noticed by Irish men and women themselves when their eyes have been opened by residence in other more orderly lands, is evident from the witty scenes in *John Bull's Other Island* when Larry Doyle brings his English friend, Broadbent, to stay under the paternal roof in Ireland. Miss Edgeworth's immortal Thady in *Castle Rackrent*, dusting down the window seat with his wig, is another example of what I mean. Of course, I know quite well that for the most part in the houses of the professional and educated classes in Ireland there is as much domestic order and beauty as could be found anywhere in the world, and I know that Irish gardens are justly celebrated all over the world ; but these things have not leavened the lump, as they have in England, and I leave it to others to try to solve the problem why this is so.

There was always a fairly strong Suffrage movement in Ireland and many of the most distinguished Irish men and women have given it invaluable support. An early article by Sir Horace Plunkett on the actual working of Women's Suffrage in Wyoming was a valuable contribution to our knowledge on the subject. We have also had on our side Mr. G. Bernard Shaw, the Rev. J. O. Hannay, Canon of St. Patrick's Cathedral, Dublin, better known by his pen-name of George A. Birmingham, Mrs. Rowan Hamilton, Miss Œnone Somerville, and Miss Violet Martin (Martin Ross), whose first book, *Experiences of an Irish R.M.*, is known and enjoyed throughout the whole English-speaking world ; it has been followed by a long series of books on Irish life inimitable in their wit and insight. These wise and witty Irish men and women belonging to all parties have given an unstinted support to the enfranchisement of women, and so have the leaders of education throughout Ireland, including Miss White, LL.D., in Dublin, Professor Hartog, of Cork, the Jewish Senior Wrangler of 1869, who had been excluded from his degree because he could not take an oath " on the true faith of a Christian," and Mrs. Byers, of Belfast. It is very greatly to the credit of the leaders of the Suffrage movement in Ireland that although the whole period of the struggle was one of fierce antagonism, amounting virtually at times to civil war, as between Home Rulers and Unionists, there was never any difficulty in arranging successful and harmonious conferences on the Suffrage question between representatives of all the parties in Ireland. Such an amount of good sense and moderation was not to be found in either England or Scotland at the time.

I have two little anecdotes to tell illustrative of the generous side of the Irish peasant character. My authority for them is Sir Henry Blake. During very troubled times in Ireland, a small expedition was sent to arrest a man charged with a serious crime ; the route lay through a desolate and lonely country, and at one point it was necessary to cross a stream. This was done without difficulty ; the man sought for was found, arrested and brought away, but when the escort arrived at the stream which had been so easily crossed a few hours back, it had become a formidable barrier, being in reality a tidal river now flowing deep and strong. When talking over alternative courses, the prisoner volunteered the information that he knew a place where the stream could be safely forded even at high water, and he volunteered to carry the whole party, one by one, on his back across it ; and this is what was actually done. No thought of treachery appeared to occur either to the prisoner or to members of the party who had arrested him.

My other story is that having had a man arrested and

punished severely for a serious crime, the magistrate and the ex-prisoner met again when the former was bent on descending a great cliff on the Donegal coast in search of sea-birds' eggs. There was one clutch of eggs the magistrate was particularly anxious to seize ; but it was inaccessible unless he was lowered on a rope from the top of the cliff. This being obvious to both men, the magistrate was lowered over the cliff until he had possessed himself of the eggs he coveted, and was safely raised to the top again, by the very man on whom he had quite recently passed a severe sentence. Again no thought of treachery occurred to either of them.

Chapter X

HOLIDAYS

I WORKED HARD when I was at work, speaking and lecturing up and down the country, writing for the magazines and for the Press, hitting the Anti-Suffragists, metaphorically, on the head, whenever opportunity offered : but my life was by no means all work. I immensely enjoyed seeing foreign countries, and for several years I spent spring or autumn holidays visiting them while my husband was fishing either in his beloved trout streams in Wiltshire or for salmon in Scotland. Switzerland and Italy were my favourite resorts, and later Germany, where over and over again I attended the Wagner festivals at Bayreuth. In Switzerland my dear brother Sam was sometimes my companion ; in Italy Emma Miller, my sister Elizabeth, my cousin B. E. Rawlins, or my sister-in-law Maria Fawcett. On one of the Swiss expeditions I induced my husband to go with me, but this was not a success. He was ordinarily so completely cheerful that I had underestimated the degree to which he would suffer in a place where hardly anything but external beauty and grandeur was spoken of ; I had extolled the mountain air, but he scoffed at it and said he preferred the shady side of Regent Street. Two of our Cambridge friends were our companions, who, of course, helped him to the utmost of their power. With one of them, Mr. J. F. Moulton (afterwards Lord Moulton), I made the ascent of Monte Rosa from the Riffel Alp, with the usual escort of guides and porters. We had perfect weather and encountered no difficulties. I immensely enjoyed the expedition, but Harry was in a fever of anxiety during every hour of my absence, and I felt on my return that I ought not to have gone.

On another holiday, in an earlier year, I made my first visit to Rome. This was in 1874. The moment when one sees Rome for the first time is as memorable as the first sight of Jerusalem. The Government of a United Italy had not very long established itself in the Eternal City, and at the time of our arrival the Chamber was sitting. The air was throbbing with political excitement and enthusiasm, but there were also many cross-currents of gossip. One piece of this gossip was that Garibaldi, who had been elected but had not taken his seat, could not, or would not, do so, because he was at heart a Republican, and therefore could not take the oath of allegiance to the King of Italy, Victor Emmanuel, il Regalantuomo. This rumour reached the ears of the grand old patriot. His real reason for not taking his seat was that he was crippled by rheumatism and could scarcely even stand without assistance. He then at once determined, whatever pain it cost him, to take his seat, and, supported on one side by his son and on the other by a friend, he had advanced up the Chamber and had taken the oath, his loud " Giuro " being heard distinctly all over the assembly. Rome was full of this incident at the time of our arrival.

We had some very kind friends—Mrs. and the Misses Morgan, the mother and sisters of Mr. H. A. Morgan, of Jesus College, Cambridge—who had spent several winters in Rome and helped us to see and hear many interesting things we should otherwise have missed. One of the greatest services they rendered us was taking us to see Garibaldi, who was then living in a villa just outside the walls. I had never been in a presence so inherently noble. He was simple and majestic, absolutely without pose or any sort of affectation. His face was very fine. I was able to give him some messages from friends of his in England, one particularly from Mrs. Charles Seely (the grandmother of the well-known bearer of that name to-day). She had entertained Garibaldi in her home in the Isle of Wight, and was also one of my very kindest friends in London. We had brought some photographs of the General with us, intending to ask him to multiply their value a thousand-fold by adding his signature to them. But when we were face to face with him this seemed an impertinence, and we refrained from asking the favour of him ; but he caught a glimpse of the photographs and said quite simply, " You would like me to sign them," and took them from us and added his signature. I quite realized in his presence what a magnetic influence he must have had over his followers in the strenuous times of his noble life. When in later years I read in Mr. G. M. Trevelyan's *Garibaldi's Defence of the Roman Republic* his last speech in the Piazza of St. Peter's before leaving Rome, defeated and a fugitive, in 1848, I could feel the thrill that must have passed through the men who were crowding round him on that day :

Fortune (he said), who betrays us to-day, will smile on us to-morrow. I am going out from Rome. Let those who wish to continue the war against the stranger, come with me. I offer neither pay, nor quarters, nor provisions : I offer hunger, thirst, forced marches, battles, and death. Let him who loves his country in his heart, and not with his lips merely, follow me.

Mr. Trevelyan goes on to describe how Garibaldi rode away through the frantic and sobbing crowd :

Above the upturned faces of those broken-hearted men and women rose the calm set features of Garibaldi, resembling a perfect type of ancient Greek beauty, and lit up with that serene and simple regard of fortitude and faith which gave him the power to lead the feebler multitudes of mortal man as though he were the sole descendant of some fable god-like race of old.[1]

---

[1] *Garibaldi's Defence of the Roman Republic*, p. 232.

It is one of my most cherished memories to have stood in that noble presence, to have heard his voice, to have pressed his hand.

It is rather an anti-climax after this to add that we also attended an audience given by the Pope, Pio Nono, a kind, stout, commonplace old gentleman, quite pleased to bring out any word or two of English when he had English visitors. " I see, Inglese very nice," and so on. My sister Elizabeth, who was of our party, had brought a rosary with her to be blessed by the Pope. This was to enhance its value for its future owner, a faithful old cook, who was a Roman Catholic. I peered about as we were being marshalled through the ante-chambers trying to identify the pictures which were painted to celebrate the massacre of St. Bartholomew, and I think I succeeded with one of them representing the murder of Gaspard de Coligny, the Admiral : the body, whether alive or dead at the moment represented is uncertain, but gaping with wounds and horribly disfigured, is being thrown from the window into the street below. When Dean Inge and others argue that human nature has no tendency to improve and remains to-day just what it was hundreds of years ago, do they take into account horrors like the St. Bartholomew massacre, which cannot be excused as an outburst of diabolical frenzy, but was planned by men and women of the highest intelligence and culture, and was applauded by the " Vicar of Christ," the representative of the Christian religion, who was enthroned in the Vatican ? Only yesterday an excellent man was heard explaining to a long-suffering audience that the devil is the master of this world. But surely Browning was nearer the truth when in *Saul* he writes :

Let one more attest !
I have lived, seen God's hand thro' a lifetime, and all was for best.

THE GENERAL ELECTIONS
OF 1874 AND 1880

M Y HUSBAND HAD BEEN DEFEATED in Brighton at the 1874 General Election. This was the election so suddenly announced by Mr. Gladstone in February, prior to which both he and Disraeli had promised, if returned to power, to abolish the income tax, leaving, needless to say, loopholes, through which they could escape if they found it inconvenient to " deliver the goods." The election completely swept away the big Liberal majority returned in 1868, and Disraeli became Prime Minister with a working majority in the House of Commons for the first time. My husband was not long out of Parliament. An old friend, Sir Charles Reade, for reasons of health and advancing years, resigned his seat for the borough of Hackney, and my husband was elected in his place by a large majority, in April 1874, and continued to represent the immense borough, then undivided and some twelve miles round, until the end of his life in 1884. It was generally recognized that his successful opposition to Mr. Gladstone's Irish University Bill had been one of the main causes of the Liberal defeat in 1874. But the existence of a Conservative Government emphasized his points of agreement with the Liberal leaders, and their relations to him consequently became less strained. He concentrated once again on his work for India and on the maintenance of Free Trade. When the Liberals were returned by a large majority in the General Election of 1880 and Mr. Gladstone was once more Prime Minister, he offered my husband a place in his Government as Postmaster-General, but without a seat in his Cabinet.

After my husband had become a member of the Government, it was pointed out to me that it would be fitting that I should be presented at Court; I therefore made my curtsey to Queen Victoria in 1881. In the autumn we were invited (my husband for the fishing) by Sir J. Mackenzie of Glenmuick to visit him in Scotland. He was quite a near neighbour of the Prince and Princess of Wales, who were then at Abergeldie; and we were twice invited there, once to dinner, quite a small family party, and once to a dance : the Prince and Princess were all that Royal hosts ought to be. He was particularly vigilant in looking after the comfort of his guests. He took me in to dinner, and I maintained the propriety and value of women being trained as doctors. H.R.H. at that time had only gone as far as wishing them to be efficient nurses. The children, the little girls only, came in at dessert, and the Prince talked to them all in turn in either English, French, or German, with equal ease and gaiety. He had the *joie de vivre* and the art of imparting it to others. At the dance Queen Victoria was present, very stately and dignified. It was a pleasure to see her dancing a reel and doing all her steps very carefully and conscientiously.

My husband threw himself into his new work at the Post Office with enthusiasm and determined within a very short time to concentrate on five important postal reforms. He worked steadily to establish (1) the parcels post, (2) postal orders, (3) sixpenny telegrams, (4) the banking of small sums by means of postage stamps, (5) giving increased facilities for life insurance and annuities. He also very considerably developed and extended the employment of women. The new Postal Order branch was placed entirely in women's hands. I remember being taken over this branch and seeing the women clerks there, and also in the Savings Bank department doing their additions of each day's transactions as quickly as they could turn the file of small pieces of thin paper containing the records. This to me was miraculous, for it was dependent on a gift in which I had not the smallest share. The postal official who took me round showed me his huge ledgers in which the accounts were entered day by day, and said to me solemnly, " There was a time, Mrs. Fawcett, when we did not think that females were capable of making figures like these." He also told me of an ingenious plan for lessening the physical labour of moving these very weighty volumes by inserting them in their stands upside down ; they could then be drawn down on to the desks without actually lifting them at all. This is an example of what I believe are many cases where male employees benefit by the devices introduced mainly on behalf of women to minimize the physical exertion needed in the daily routine of work : men are just as human as women, and it is undesirable to overtax their strength when it can be easily avoided.

My husband soon developed cordial and even affectionate relations with those officers, whether high or low in the G.P.O., who were most in contact with him, from the messengers to the permanent secretaries, engineers, electricians, and solicitors, for he had the same power of sympathy with their point of view and appreciation of work well done. He had, moreover, the open mind on questions relating to any suggested reform, always ready to give all the arguments, pro and con, full consideration. He never allowed anyone to be dismissed without careful personal investigation : he was particularly careful in filling up vacancies, such as occur in the postmasterships in towns whether small or great, never to allow political considerations to influence the appointments. He had almost a quarrel with a vehement and masterful politician because he had insisted when filling a postal appointment in a town, of which the politician was an uncrowned king, to consider nothing but the professional record of the applicants. When his death took place after a brief illness in 1884, there was a remarkable demonstration of grief and affection from the whole of the great staff. One of them wrote, " The humblest servant within the dominion of his authority was not left uncared for. During his history as Postmaster-General a greatly improved state of feeling has been introduced among the officers in their general tone towards each other and towards those beneath them, and the whole service has been greatly and wonderfully improved." [1] A little while after his death the officials who had been most closely associated with him combined in sending me a present of eighteenth-century silver candlesticks and an inkstand as a token of " affectionate remembrance of a beloved chief." I need not say that I treasured them very much, and, of course, never should have parted with them if it had not been that in April 1916, during the darkest time of the Great War, there was an appeal, which I felt to be irresistible, from the British Red Cross to the whole country, and everyone was urged, even if he or she could not give cash, to give other possessions ; and a great sale was held at Christie's to dispose of these. This is where I sent my candlesticks and inkstand, and I felt sure my husband would have approved of this disposal of them.

My husband was only four and a half years in office, but it was long enough to make him, as well as myself, understand what people mean when they say, " There

[1] *Life of Henry Fawcett,* by Leslie Stephen, p. 446.

are only two happy days in office, the day when you accept it and the day when you leave it." It seemed to me that his superiors in the Governmental hierarchy went out of their way to slight him ; for instance, he had worked hard for the introduction of sixpenny telegrams, but when the Cabinet had at length consented to their introduction, no intimation to this effect was made to him. When the announcement was made from the Treasury Bench in the House of Commons, it was as much a surprise to him as if he had had nothing to do with making it possible. I remember his coming home to me and saying, " I would never have dreamed of treating the humblest servant in such a way." But as regards misunderstandings between my husband and Mr. Gladstone, no doubt they arose from the two men being fundamentally different. On the question of Women's Suffrage, for instance, my husband had given it a steady support ; Mr. Gladstone had been, so to speak, " all over the place " about it. In 1871 he had taken part in a Suffrage debate in the House and had said " that our law in the matters where the peculiar relations of men and women are concerned . . . does less than justice to women, and great mischief, misery, and scandal result from that state of things . . . and if it should be found possible to arrange a safe and well-adjusted alteration of the law as to political power, the man who shall attain that object and shall see his purpose carried forward to its consequences in a more full arrangement of the provisions of other laws bearing upon the condition and welfare of women, will, in my opinion, be a real benefactor of his country." Now, though it was obviously impossible to say what this strange medley meant, it was generally thought to mean that Mr. Gladstone believed that women had suffered practical grievances from their want of electoral power, and that it would be for their benefit and for the welfare of the country if a moderate measure of Women's Suffrage could be passed into law. In the same debate Sir Henry James, afterwards Lord James of Hereford, showed that he believed this was Mr. Gladstone's meaning, and made a bitter attack upon him in consequence.

However, Mr. Gladstone did not come out as a decided opponent of Women's Suffrage until later than this. In his first Midlothian Campaign in 1879, he urged the then voteless women of the constituency to engage and bear an active part in the great struggle, " which so far (he said) from involving any departure from your character as women . . . would serve to gild your future years with sweet remembrances and to warrant you in hoping that, each in your own place and sphere, has raised her voice for justice, and has striven to mitigate the sorrows and misfortunes of mankind." He could not for long maintain his balance on these lofty heights ; for a few years later he was writing a letter for publication to a well-known Anti-Suffragist M.P., Mr. Samuel Smith, to say that he feared voting would injure women, " would trespass upon their delicacy, their purity, their refinement, the elevation of their whole nature." And when in 1884 his own Reform Bill was before the House, and Mr. Woodall, M.P., had moved an amendment which would have extended its provisions to women, Mr. Gladstone opposed the amendment with passion. If there had been ambiguity in his expressions in 1871, there was none whatever in 1884. He said : " I offer it " (Mr. Woodall's Women's Suffrage Amendment) " the strongest opposition in my power, and I must disclaim and renounce all responsibility for the measure (i.e. the Government Reform Bill) should my honourable friend succeed in inducing the Committee to adopt the amendment." Of course the amendment was heavily defeated, by 271 votes to 135 : of the 271 members who voted against it there were 104 Liberals who had pledged themselves to support the enfranchisement of women. That division probably sowed the seed of the militant movement. It certainly produced a deep feeling of anger and distrust among the women who were devoting themselves to the Suffrage movement. I bring the matter in here because of the illustration which it gives of the relations between my husband and Mr. Gladstone. My husband did not vote at all ; he and two other members of the Government walked out before the division. The next day he received a letter in Mr. Gladstone's own hand pointing out that to abstain from supporting a Government in a critical division was equivalent to a resignation of office. With this letter was enclosed a memorandum, signed by himself, stating that a crisis in foreign affairs was approaching " which might be of the deepest importance to the character and honour of the country and to the law, the concord, and possibly even to the peace of Europe. . . . It would be most unfortunate at such a juncture were the minds of men to be disturbed by the resignation of a Cabinet Minister and of two other gentlemen holding offices of great importance. . . . I therefore propose to my colleagues that I be authorized to request the President of the Local Government Board, the Postmaster-General, and the Secretary to the Treasury, that they will do us the favour to retain their respective offices." My husband replied quite respectfully that he had not abstained from voting on Mr. Woodall's amendment until he had duly weighed in all their bearings the consequences which such a course of action might involve. But he did not go through the form of withdrawing a resignation which he had never tendered.

But there was another crack of the whip by his superiors in Governmental rank which caused him much greater annoyance. It was a time of the fiercest fighting

between the Irish Party and the Government. Mr.
Gladstone had lately said in reference to Mr. Parnell
and his followers " that they were marching through
rapine to the dismemberment of the Empire," and had
also said that the resources of civilization, in dealing
with the situation thus created, had not been exhausted.
One of these " resources of civilization " was the opening
of the letters of the Irish members as they passed through
the Post Office. To this my husband strongly objected,
but he was reminded in no gentle terms by Sir William
Harcourt, then Home Secretary, that he, my husband,
had no authority in the matter, that as the head in the
Home Office he had decided that the letters should be
opened. My husband again remonstrated in person to
Sir William Harcourt, and by letter to Mr. Gladstone,
but in vain. All this was well known at the time ;
the occasion was celebrated in the House of Commons
by jokes and verses from Sir Wilfrid Lawson, and by
a question from Mr. T. D. Sullivan. The main political
result of this violation of private correspondence was
the intensifying of the hatred with which the Parnellite
Party regarded Mr. Gladstone : they issued an official
manifesto denouncing the Liberal Party as " perfidious,
treacherous, and incompetent," also " as a servile and
cowardly herd." What, then, was my amusement
when in January 1887 an article appeared in the
Nineteenth Century written by Mr. Gladstone on Locksley
Hall and the Jubilee, in which he called attention to
the vast improvement which had taken place in manners
and morals at the time of writing compared with fifty
years earlier. At that time, half a century ago, he
wrote : " The Government, at its discretion, opened,
when it chose to see cause, letters confided to the Post
Office. *This bad practice has died out.*" The italics are
mine. I disclosed the facts in a letter to *The Times*,
to which no reply, so far as I can remember, was ever

made. It is difficult to see what reply could have been made. I did not go one inch beyond the facts ; moreover, the proof of them lay, and still lies, in my possession. A curious little sidelight on Mr. Gladstone's retentive memory in some matters may be inferred from the fact that at the time of my husband's death in 1884, though I received hundreds of letters of sympathy and condolence from all sorts and conditions of people, I received not one word from the Prime Minister under whom he had served.

EARLY SUFFRAGE WORK: SOWING SEED

I N ONE OF THE BIOGRAPHIES of Abraham Lincoln
it is told how, when a young man, he visited New
Orleans and saw the slave-market there in full activity,
a going concern. "He saw a young mulatto girl
exposed naked before the buyers and handled by them
as if she were an animal . . . one of his companions
declared that Lincoln burst out, ' My God, boys, let
us get away from this. If ever I get a chance to hit
that thing, I'll hit it hard.' " The biographer states
that the effect of this incident upon Lincoln's thought
and feeling throughout his subsequent career could be
easily traced.[1]

I am very far from comparing myself with Abraham
Lincoln, or of comparing the legal and social subjection
of women in England in the nineteenth century with
the gross horrors of the slave trade in its most terrible
aspects. Nevertheless, I confess to having been very
much moved to devote myself to gaining political and
social equality for the women of my own country by
two small accidentally heard conversations between
women. One took place in my own home before my
marriage and the second after it, in the waiting-room
at Ipswich station. Imagine, then, Alde House packed
to its greatest capacity for a dance ; three in a bedroom
with a fire, and two of our guests and myself sitting over

---

[1] See *Abraham Lincoln*, by F. I. Paradise (Mills & Boon, London), p. 23.

it before dressing for the dance. I was by far the youngest of the three. My two companions were talking, and presently took up the subject of the failure of a recent marriage in our immediate circle. The young husband and wife were estranged, and no one exactly knew the reason why ; after pursuing this interesting theme for some time, one said to the other, " I cannot see what she has to complain of. *Look how he dresses her !* " I fumed inwardly, but said nothing. I thought I would like to try to make that sort of talk impossible. I kept on thinking about it, and the shame and degradation of it, which seemed to be accepted by my companions as a matter of course. I did not know anything at that time about " kept women," but " Look how he dresses her " was of its essence.

The other conversation which greatly influenced me was in the waiting-room at Ipswich station, and was between two clergymen's wives, who were busy making small articles of lace, which were to be sold for the benefit of the schools in their respective parishes. " What do you find sells best ? " said No. 1 to No. 2, who instantly replied, " *Oh ! things that are really useful, such as butterflies for the hair !* " Of course there was a comic aspect to this which I did not fail to appreciate, but I hoped a time would come before very long when intelligent and active-minded women would cease to regard " butterflies for the hair " as " really useful."

What I have already written explains, I hope, how it was that from quite early youth I worked continuously for Women's Suffrage, first as a member of Mrs. P. A. Taylor's committee in 1867, and afterwards until we won the vote in 1918. It was, of course, obvious that work for political freedom represented only one phase of a many-sided movement. Speaking generally, its most important departments dealt with (1) education,

(2) an equal moral standard between men and women, (3) professional and industrial liberty, and (4) political status. My special experience and training fitted me best, as I thought, for work on behalf of the fourth of these, but I recognized that this was only one side of the whole question, and I was likewise convinced that whoever worked for any of the branches of our movement was, whether he knew it or not, really helping on the other three. I was ready with any help I was able to give to these, whilst concentrating for my own special part upon the fourth.

My leaders on the education question were Miss Davies, Professor Henry Sidgwick, Mrs. William Grey, and Miss Mary Gurney ; on the equal moral standard they were Mrs. Josephine Butler, Dr. Elizabeth Blackwell, Sir James Stansfeld, and Professor Stuart ; on professional and industrial freedom, my sister Elizabeth and Miss Jessie Boucherett, the former leading the claim of women to professional, while the latter was championing their claim to industrial, freedom. .

The history of the early years of the work for opening up avenues of industrial employment for women would form curious reading now ; it is embodied to a large extent in the reports of the Society for Promoting the Employment of Women. This society, founded in 1859, is still flourishing and active ; but in the sixty-four years of its history it has seen almost a complete revolution in the direction which has been its constant object to promote. In its earlier years it had to convince the public that, for instance, the dressing of ladies' hair was an occupation not beyond the powers of an average woman. " Impossible, madam," said a male hairdresser to my sister Louie, " it took ME a fortnight to learn it." What would people of this type have thought if they could have seen women acting successfully as omnibus conductors, gardeners, engineers, doctors, lawyers, auctioneers, bank clerks, glaziers, librarians, indexers, etc.? As I am writing this page I see in the *Woman's Leader*, 23rd November 1923, a paragraph describing the greatly increased activity of women in commerce ; while in *The Times* of the same date it is noted that the French Senate had recently adopted, without discussion, a proposal that auctioneers' *commissaires priseurs* in France shall in future be nominated without distinction of sex. The same paragraph calls attention to the fact that the woman auctioneer is already in existence in England ; and that Miss Barlow acts in this capacity on behalf of the firm of Messrs. Sotheby. The newspapers record almost daily the increasing activity of women of all classes of society in business. The thing is marching by itself, and no longer needs external props.

When I first began Suffrage work one of my chief colleagues and helpers was Lilias Ashworth (afterwards Mrs. Hallett), of Bath, a niece of Mr. John Bright and also of Mrs. MacLaren, of Edinburgh. Lily Ashworth was one of two beautiful sisters, orphans, " richly left,'" or what was considered so in those days. They had been brought up as Quakers, and they dressed with exquisite care in the rich simplicity, but not in the style of the sect to which they still belonged. Both were delicately fair, with hair the colour of undyed floss silk. They had a charming house, Claverton Lodge, on Bathwick Hill, where we rested after our Suffrage journeys in what was to me unwonted luxury and comfort. We were told that the fashionable young men of Bath used to assemble outside the door of the Quakers' Meeting House on Sundays to see these two beautiful sisters enter. Anne, the elder of the two, never spoke or took part in public work of any kind. But she helped and supported the movement in every other way in her power. It was delightful, coming back, after a round of sometimes dusty, rowdy meetings, to the quiet and luxurious comfort of the home which Anne created at Claverton Lodge. We had, from the first, a good deal of support in the West Country. F. W. Newman, the brother of the more famous Cardinal John Henry Newman, was a staunch supporter. He had become a Unitarian, and brought our movement under the favourable consideration of the Unitarian body. Among other supporters in the West of England I may mention the poet, T. E. Brown, then a master at Clifton College. Dr. Percival, the head master, afterwards the Bishop of Hereford (Dr. Percival and I became co-trustees for a Working Women's Benefit Society at Bristol), Helen Blackburn, later our invaluable secretary in London, was in these early Suffrage years living in Bristol, where she had much influence and brought us the sympathetic support of numbers of the most distinguished residents, among them the Sturges, the Tanners, Dr. and Mrs. Beddoes, and many others. From 1868 a real Suffrage organization began to grow up in the country. Its chief centres were London, Manchester, Birmingham, Bristol, and Edinburgh. In London our leaders were, besides Mrs. Peter Taylor, Miss Davies, my sister, Mrs. Anderson, Miss Ashurst Biggs, Mr. Shaen, Mr. Stansfeld, and Mme. Bodichon (Barbara Leigh Smith). In Manchester we were led by Miss Becker, Mr. and Mrs. Jacob Bright, and Mr. John Thomasson the elder ; in Birmingham, by Mr. and Mrs. Osler and the Sturge family. The Bristol leaders I have already named : while in Edinburgh we had a brilliant group of men and women among whom we counted Professor Masson, the author of the monumental Life of John Milton; Mrs. MacLaren, sister of John Bright and wife of the member for the City of Edinburgh; Lady Strachey, wife of Sir Richard Strachey, and herself a Grant of Rothiemurchus and a very active Suffrage missionary ;

Miss S. S. Mair (the initials S. S. stand for Sarah Siddons, she is a great-granddaughter and a worthy descendant of the great actress); and the Misses Stevenson, whose house in Randolph Crescent was the headquarters of all kinds of active work for opening new opportunities for women. I once asked Sir Johnston Forbes-Robertson, who did such active service for our cause in its later stages, how he had been converted to Suffrage; he answered that he had never needed conversion; he was a born Suffragist, and he said, with a smile, that he must have contracted Suffrage views in his infancy from his godfather, Professor Masson.

It will be in the remembrance of some of my readers that our first Suffrage success in the House of Commons was won by Mr. Jacob Bright in 1870. He had charge of a Women's Suffrage Bill in that year, and got a second reading for it by 124 to 91 votes, but further progress was blocked by the Liberal leaders. In 1869 Mr. Jacob Bright had also succeeded in passing, in all its stages in both Houses of Parliament, a Bill to open the Local Government Franchise to women. The next year saw the passing of the first important Government Education Act; and Mr. W. E. Foster, who had charge of it, though an opponent of the political franchise for women, embodied in his Act a clause giving them the education franchise and also rendering them eligible to sit upon the newly created School Boards. From this time forth all local representative bodies in the United Kingdom were elected by the male and female ratepayers of each place, and the disqualification of sex gradually disappeared from the local government electorate. When some people make the assertion that we worked for Women's Suffrage for nearly fifty years without making any progress, they forget these things that were really of the utmost importance in paving the way for victory in wider areas.

Another of the events of 1870 indicates the hold which the principle of equality between men and women had made at that time. The elections for the first School Boards took place in 1870. The women who were returned were the very same women who were most identified with the movement for Parliamentary Suffrage, namely, Miss Elizabeth Garrett, M.D. (afterwards Mrs. Anderson), and Miss Davies for Marylebone and Greenwich respectively; Miss Becker, for Manchester; and Miss Flora Stevenson, for Edinburgh. Miss Garrett had an immense majority in the big, undivided borough of Marylebone. It was said at the time, and I think it is probably true even now, that she polled more votes than had ever been bestowed on any candidate in any election in Great Britain. The number was over 47,000. She and Miss Davies, Miss Becker, and Miss Flora Stevenson had all identified themselves with Suffrage work. Miss Becker retained her seat for Manchester until her death in 1890, and Miss Flora Stevenson was also continuously re-elected for thirty-three years until her death in 1905. She acted as convener of some of the most important committees of the Board; she constantly came up to London on their behalf to transact Parliamentary and other business, and was unanimously elected their Chairman in 1900. Miss Rosamund Davenport-Hill, another prominent Suffragist, sat for many years as member for the City of London on the London School Board. All these things prove, I believe, beyond doubt that the general good sense of the electors endorsed the value of women's services in public work, and that the man in the street was entirely unconvinced by the Anti-Suffrage talk about the " immeasurable injury of bringing women into the conflict of political life." An amusing aspect of the controversy was found in the fact that the very same ladies who stated with so much emphasis that women were totally unfit to take part in political life were always ready to take part in it themselves ; they wrote and spoke on political platforms, canvassed electors, published election literature, and even started classes intended to train young women in the art of speaking, so that they should be able to proclaim on public platforms that " woman's place is home." One of the more active of these Anti-Suffrage orators had written and published as follows : " For social purposes, now and always, Man is superior to Woman. Organized society rests on him. It would go on quite comfortably if every woman retired to her own wigwam and did nothing but breed." As soon as Suffrage was carried, however, this lady offered herself for a seat in a Colonial Parliament, and was elected ! There was no real sincerity, no conviction, in the stuff they talked on what they erroneously conceived to be the winning side. I make an exception of Mrs. Humphry Ward, for she was so constituted as to be able to believe at one and the same time that women were fundamentally incapable of taking a useful part in politics, but that she herself was an exception to the rule, for she took a deep interest in the whole political life of her country as it developed before her, and sought, both by speech and by writing, often with considerable effect, to influence its direction.

At the same time, it can easily be conceived how useful the Suffrage workers found the frothy nonsense of which a specimen has just been quoted, for it continually provided our speakers with telling illustrations of the weakness of the Anti-Suffrage case.

With our five centres in London, Bristol, Birmingham, Manchester, and Edinburgh, and the work which each was doing in forming societies and influencing opinion in its own neighbourhood, we had, as it were, the framework ready made of what afterwards became the " National Union of Women's Suffrage Societies " ;

but this did not come into actual existence until later. Our five chief societies soon learned the importance, indeed the necessity, of joint Parliamentary action, and we practised the art of working together before we formulated the rules for doing so. My speaking was done from the 'seventies onward, chiefly in connection with these large societies ; a group of meetings would be arranged in a given geographical area, and the obvious economy in labour, and also in railway fares, recommended the plan to us all. My work with my husband prevented me from giving as much time to speaking as I did later ; it was not until the 'nineties of the last century that I really made it my chief occupation. Of course one gets (at least, I got) frightfully weary of constant speaking on the same subject, and I had to refuse to speak more than once a day or more than four times a week. I tried to get home for week-ends, not always successfully. I could not have spoken as continuously as I did without long rests, and, as it was, I could only do it for about four months in the year—February and March, October and November. My pleasures and refreshments were from various sources. I formed intimate friendships with delightful people all over the country. Moreover, the great poets were ever with us : Chaucer, Shakespeare, Keats, Shelley, the Brownings, and later, many of the moderns, such as Flecker, Rupert Brooke, and Walter de la Mare ; and I also enjoyed to the full the relaxation of foreign travel. In this way I have seen the main places in the world whence our own roots have been nourished. Rome, Naples and Sicily, Athens, Egypt, and, later, Palestine. It is of incalculable interest to look into " the rock whence ye are hewn and to the pit whence ye are digged." And these excursions were not without their usefulness to the main purpose of my life. For instance, I noticed in those countries, where the type of civilization placed women on the very lowest rung of the ladder of freedom, so far from their womanly duties being better performed than with us, they were infinitely worse performed ; an Egyptian mother, I noticed, would allow her infant's face and eyes to be covered with flies and never even raise her hand to brush them off.

Chapter XIII

GREAT VICTORIES IN 1883, 1885, AND 1886

THESE WERE NOTABLE YEARS in the history of the women's movement. In 1883, after long and intensive work in the country, carried on with never-failing devotion and thoroughness, Josephine Butler had her first great victory in her campaign against the C.D. Acts. The operation of these Acts was suspended by Parliament in 1883, and they were totally repealed in 1886. A vivid report of the scene in the House of Commons on the earlier date is contained in the *Life of Josephine Butler*, by G. W. and L. A. Johnson, pp. 170–85.

Mrs. Butler and her more active workers, on the night the division was expected, had hired a room close to Palace Yard, and here they kept up continuous prayer for the success of Mr. Hopwood's motion condemning the Acts. A venerable lady from America rose at this prayer meeting and said, " Tears are good, prayers are better, but we should get on better if behind every tear there was a vote at the ballot-box." A little earlier, John Morley had entered the House for the first time to take his seat after his election for Newcastle. Mrs. Butler alludes to this in a letter to her son, saying that the first thing he did, after taking the oath, was to sit down by Mr. Hopwood and say, " Now tell me what I can do to help you to-night, for the thing our Newcastle electors were most positive about was that I should oppose this legislation." There was a most strenuous worker in Newcastle against the C.D. Acts, Mrs. Spence Watson, whom John Morley knew intimately. Years after, when the expression " The beauty of holiness " was used in his presence, he remarked that he did not know exactly how to define it, but he recognized it when he saw it in the face of Mrs. Spence Watson. (See *Quarterly Review* article on Lord Morley, January 1924.) When the day of the actual fight in the House came, in 1883, Mrs. Butler was sitting almost breathless in the Ladies' Gallery, when the Steward of the Gallery crept quietly behind her chair and whispered, " I think you are going to win." Such a course was most unusual, as the officers of the House are supposed never to show any political bias or to belong to any party ; nevertheless, Mrs. Butler says she could see the irrepressible pleasure on the man's face when he said this. The figures in support of the motion condemning compulsory examination were 182 to 110. The actual repeal of the Acts, as already related, took place in 1886. Mrs. Butler's victory was due to her own spiritual power and her capacity for awakening it in others, both men and women ; therefore, although, of course, at that time there were no women voters, the men of the country in large numbers had taken an active part in her crusade against the Acts, and there were consequently many M.P.'s who, whatever their own personal opinions might be, were constrained to vote for the suspension, and three years later for the repeal, of the Acts. Mr. Hopwood said that, as the division approached, several members came to him and said they must vote with him although their own feelings with regard to the Acts were unchanged.

One said, " It is a strange thing that people care so much about this question. All my leading constituents have asked me to vote with you." Another, a military man, said, " Well, you have extraordinary support from the country ; it is evident that yours is the winning side." The victory, however, always seems to me the most miraculous ever won in Parliament. "The Principalities and Powers and the rulers of the darkness of this world" were all against Mrs. Butler. But she justified the great passage here in part quoted, in that she took upon her "the whole armour of God and was able to stand in the evil day, and, having done all, to stand."

Mrs. Butler's victory was an immense encouragement to us ; for her task had been immeasurably more difficult than ours, and her triumph helped us to believe that all things were possible. I think her victory also had its part in promoting the success of Mr. W. T. Stead's crusade in 1885. In the summer of that year the whole world was thrilled and shaken by the publication in the *Pall Mall Gazette* of a series of articles called *The Maiden Tribute of Modern Babylon*. They were written by the editor, Mr. Stead, and with all the skill and force of an accomplished journalist exposed the horrors which were then daily and nightly taking place in London ; the sale of young girls for the purposes of prostitution. There was a howl of rage from some sections of Society, and a cry of thankfulness and hope from others, which perceived that if these horrors were to be coped with successfully they must first be made known. Stead was an Imperialist, but, as he defined the term himself, his Imperialism was an Imperialism of responsibility, an Imperialism based on common sense and the Ten Commandments.

Now for several years good men in both Houses of Parliament had been trying to pass a Criminal Law Amendment Bill, giving additional protection to young children. The age of consent at that time was only thirteen, one of the infamous facilities for wrongdoing allowed by the then existing law. Lord Shaftesbury was the moving spirit in the committee of the House of Lords which had considered the subject and had drafted an amending Bill. He had successfully piloted this Bill through all its stages in the Upper House in 1884, only to see it wrecked in the House of Commons, where it was talked out, counted out, and finally destroyed. The same process appeared to be imminent in 1885. The then City Chamberlain, Mr. Benjamin Scott, accompanied by Mrs. Josephine Butler, went to Mr. Stead and implored his help. He said he would inquire into the facts and see what could be done. Mr. Gladstone's Government had just been defeated, and a new Conservative Government was in power. It so happened that Mr. Stead had a personal friend in this Government. He consulted this friend, and asked, " Was there any chance of the new Government taking up the Bill and carrying it ? " The answer was decisive and emphatic : " Not the slightest."

Then Stead went to the head of the Criminal Investigation Department, Sir Howard Vincent, and inquired about the facts. Was it possible, he said, that wretched parents should sell their girl children when turned thirteen for the express purpose of prostitution, and that there was nothing in the law to prevent it ? Sir Howard replied that it was perfectly possible and of frequent occurrence. Stead burst out, " It is enough to rouse Hell," to which Sir Howard replied, " It does not even rouse the neighbours." Stead there and then determined it should rouse all England, and he himself undertook to simulate the purchaser of such a child, protecting himself and the child by the presence of witnesses of unimpeachable character who were able to prove that the child had been cared for and her safety protected all through, and then to tell her story, as perhaps only he could tell it, of how a little girl just turned thirteen could be bought and sold for prostitution in Christian England without let or hindrance from the law. This narrative he published in the *Pall Mall Gazette*; the story came out daily from 6th to 12th July 1885. The effect was instantaneous and world-wide. The articles set all London and the whole country in a blaze of indignation. The Bill, which a few weeks previously the Government had said they could not touch, and was consequently regarded as hopeless, was now revised and strengthened and passed into law with the utmost despatch. One man, single-handed, had coerced an unwilling legislature and a reluctant Ministry. But Stead's enemies—and they were many—were determined on revenge. In the course of his crusade he had withdrawn a little girl from her home without her father's consent: the mother's consent did not count; the father's consent had never been asked. It mattered nothing that the child had been protected and sheltered at every turn from any possible evil befalling her. Stead was believed to have broken the law, and could, and should, bear the penalty. The jury found Stead guilty, but on pronouncing their verdict, added that they recommended him to mercy, as they wished to put on record their high appreciation of the services he had rendered the nation by securing the passage of a much-needed law for the protection of young girls. This also availed nothing; he was sentenced to three months' imprisonment as an ordinary criminal. [It was afterwards proved that the child in question had been born out of wedlock, and that therefore, whoever her father was, he had no legal rights over her.] There was a tremendous outburst of public indignation at this outrageous sentence. Stead alone was tranquil and happy. He wrote to Dr. Clifford from prison : " I am full of joy as to the present, and of hope and confidence as to the future." He sent out Christmas cards bearing the words, " God, even my God, hath anointed me with the oil of gladness above my fellows." All the details of this wonderful series of events should be read in Miss Estelle Stead's little book, entitled *My Father* (Nelson & Sons). In the meantime, Stead's friends were not idle. A defence fund of several thousand pounds was raised. Public meetings of protest against the sentence were held. I took the unusual step of writing to Sir Henry Ponsonby, Queen Victoria's Private Secretary, asking that Her Majesty should give orders that while Stead was in prison he should receive the treatment of a first-class misdemeanant. In the course of my letter I said : " I yesterday saw the Rev. B. Waugh, after he had had an interview with Mr. Stead in prison. Mr. Stead was in the ordinary cotton prison dress, and appeared to be extremely cold (the date was 12th November 1885). His cell is very dark ; it contains a Bible, but the cell is so dark it is impossible to read it. . . . He was very cheerful when Mr. Waugh saw him, and complains of nothing and desires his friends not to complain for him. The warder treats him with respect and kindness. His being thus subjected to ordinary prison discipline will be the more noticeable because Mr. Valentine Baker and Mr. Edmund Yates during their terms of imprisonment were treated as first-class misdemeanants."

Sir Henry Ponsonby replied from Balmoral without delay : " I was certainly surprised to read in the newspapers the statements relating to Mr. Stead's imprisonment, and I can understand your writing on the subject." He then proceeded to explain to me the constitutional position (of which I was not ignorant), namely, that Her Majesty could take no political action without the advice of her Secretary of State. But his letter continued : " As soon as I received your letter, I telegraphed to the Secretary of State, and was glad to receive a reply from him this evening that Mr. Stead had been placed in a higher class and would therefore be saved from the severe treatment he at first received." I felt deeply thankful for this friendly and prompt action.

The deep interest and the intense indignation aroused by what we all believed to be a plot against Stead, intended to penalize him for one of the best actions which a man could perform, did not die down because the intended victim had become a first-class misdemeanant. Indignation meetings were held which Mrs. Josephine Butler and Mrs. Booth, wife of General Booth, of the Salvation Army, addressed, and at which I took a subordinate part. On the afternoon of a day fixed for a Stead Defence Meeting in Exeter Hall, at which I had promised to speak, I had a call from our old friend Mr. Auberon Herbert. I did not see him, for it was the late afternoon, and I had gone to lie down in preparation for the evening meeting. He apparently feared that this meant that I was not coming, and he sent me up an urgent message. I scribbled a note : " Dear Mr. Herbert, if I am alive I shall be there." Though he probably did not know it, this was an exact reproduction of his own reply a few years earlier to my husband, who was urging him not to risk his life by facing the Jingo crowd in Hyde Park, which was then (1877) backing the Turk against the Russian. He had already had one marvellous escape from the mob, which had chased him down to the Serpentine and would have had great pleasure in drowning him in it. His wife and sister had been quite unsuccessful in urging him not to risk his life by repeating the experiment. These ladies thought my husband might succeed where they had failed, so Harry got Mr. Herbert into a quiet corner and poured out every argument at his command to induce him to desist, pointing out that a man with a wife and young children should not expose himself to assault and possible death where no practical good was likely to result. Mr. Herbert listened in silence, and when my husband paused for a moment, said in the quietest, gentlest voice, "Dear Fawcett, if I am alive I shall be there."

The enthusiasm roused by Stead's revelations did not burn itself out in empty denunciations, whether of rage or vengeance. It had permanent results. The National Vigilance Association was formed and practically led for the rest of his life by a very remarkable man, Mr. W. A. Coote, formerly a compositor on the *Standard* newspaper. He had extraordinary gifts for the work he had undertaken, an unbounded faith in goodness, unfailing good manners, making his appeal always to what was highest and best in men and women. He was as wonderful in his way as Stead was in his. His organization, national at first, gradually became international, and much of the good work now being done internationally through the League of Nations in restricting and preventing the Traffic in Women and Children had its root and origin in the work done by W. A. Coote and the Association of which he was the life and soul. (For up-to-date information on this point see *The Vigilance Record*, March 1924.)

Chapter XIV

ILLNESS AND DEATH OF
HENRY FAWCETT, 1884

M Y HUSBAND had had a severe illness in 1882 ; but he recovered mainly through the exertions of a number of devoted doctors and other friends, among whom I must mention Sir Andrew Clark, my sister Elizabeth, and Dr. Ford Anderson, among the physicians ; and my sister Agnes, Louise Wilkinson (afterwards my sister-in-law), and Margaret Cowie, who gave to me and him extraordinary help and affection.

Although he recovered in 1882, my husband did not regain his former perfect health ; and in 1884, almost exactly two years after his first illness, he was struck down by a sudden attack of pneumonia, and died after a few days' illness on 6th November, at the age of fifty-one. I need not dwell on what this meant to me, and how it altered my whole life.

The sympathy I received from the entire country touched me profoundly. My husband was a man who inspired deep and lasting affection in all who knew him. There was something heroic in the gay courage with which he bore his blindness that made a universal appeal.

Queen Victoria wrote me a letter in her own hand to express her sorrow and sympathy, and also her appreciation of his services to his country. The Prince of

Wales (afterwards Edward VII) also wrote a very warm-hearted letter. The staff and employees of the Post Office made me feel that they had lost a chief whom they really loved. His services to India are to this day affectionately remembered after nearly forty years. His friends put up a beautiful sculptured memorial to him in Westminster Abbey. It is in the old baptistery, sometimes called the little poet's corner, for it also contains monuments to Wordsworth, Matthew Arnold, Charles Kingsley, as well as windows in memory of George Herbert and Cowper. The inscription for the Abbey memorial of my husband was written by his friend Leslie Stephen. The concluding passage runs thus :

> His heroic acceptance of the calamity of blindness
> Has left a memorable example of the power of a
> Brave man to transmute evil into good and to
> Wrest victory from misfortune.

Besides this memorial in the Abbey there are three other memorials in London, and others in Salisbury, Cambridge, Aldeburgh, and Trumpington. In enumerating them in the *Life* of my husband, Mr. Stephen concluded his memoir with these words :

> Such monuments are but the outward symbols of the living influence still exercised upon the hearts of his countrymen by a character equally remarkable for masculine independence and generous sympathy. My sole aim has been to do something towards enabling my readers to bring that influence to bear upon themselves.[1]

Left alone after seventeen years of happy active married life, having been the partner and friend of my husband, sharing in all his activities (except fishing, which I could never endure), I might have fallen into a lethargic melancholy if it had not been for the help I received from many of my husband's old friends, and also in a very high degree from all the members of my own

---

[1] *Life of Henry Fawcett*, by Leslie Stephen (Smith Elder), p. 468.

family, father, mother, sisters, brothers, and also from my own daughter. These all stood by me and helped me at every turn. My brother Sam, of whom, of course, I had seen a great deal during his undergraduate life at Cambridge, then became the first and foremost among my men friends. His was a remarkable character, for he possessed a wonderful combination of qualities : first-rate brain-power, an absolutely selfless nature, a keen appreciation of public duty, and added to all these a strong sense of humour, which made me save up every amusing incident I met with in order that I might tell him and hear his explosion of hearty laughter. Sam's second son, born about a year after my husband's death, was named after him, Henry Fawcett. He was my godson, and I watched with special interest the development of his strong and lovable character. He became an artist by profession, and had already shown great promise when his life was cut short in the Great War. He fell at Gallipoli in September 1915, one of the ten dear young men, sons, sons-in-law, nephews, and cousins, who were lost to our family through the war.

After my widowhood, Sam became among my brothers my closest friend and adviser, while Agnes occupied this place among my sisters. We three were as nearly as may be of an age. We had had our youth together, a very strong bond. Agnes, in 1882, had lost her dearly loved friend and house-mate through the death of our cousin Rhoda. We had thus each received a heavy stroke of personal sorrow, and it seemed very natural that we should henceforth live together, and make our joint home in her house. My Cambridge home was broken up, and my London home, with its pleasant garden, was only a shadow of what it had been ; but I had always loved the Gower Street house and all its associations, and so had Philippa, who had been as much devoted to Agnes and Rhoda as a child could be.

Chapter XV

PHILIPPA AT CAMBRIDGE

U P TO THE PRESENT I have told little of Philippa, but, of course, this is not because I remember little. At first, when she was a baby girl, I delighted in her rapidly developing mind, in her curiosity, and in her quaint expressions. She was always asking " Why ? " Someone at Cambridge said to her, " Do you always say ' Why,' Philippa ? " She replied, " No, sometimes I say ' Why, oh ! why ? ' " Her " why " often took me out of my depth. For instance, she would ask, " Why was it wrong to be cross, to tell lies ? " and so on ; and I started trying to explain that, in the matter of truthfulness, for example, if we couldn't depend on one another all satisfaction and happiness in one's life would be gone. Then she continued, " If I told lies would you leave off loving me ? " This was rather a poser, and I fenced. " Well, no, not at once, of course : but if you went on telling lies and being cross, I should not love you so much, and gradually, perhaps, I should leave off loving you altogether." Then she looked up, and said, " Would you ? Well, I should love you if you was ever so naughty." I felt that she had thoroughly bested me, and that we had better have a game or run races on the Trumpington road. Once, on this same road, we met a nurse wheeling a perambulator, and Philippa piped out " I know that person in that perambulator." Of course I laughed, but she gave no explanation until quite a long time after, when she said that if she had used the word " baby " it would have implied that she did not know she was a baby herself. One of her questions asked of her nurse was, " What was the real colour of the flowers ? Was it the colour they seemed to have when the sun shone on them, or was it the colour they looked when it was cloudy ? " Her droll expressions and thoughts were a constant pleasure to us. Like many other children, she always had an hour sacred to herself just before our dinner, and she intensely resented callers at this time. Once, when a very great friend, Dr. Henry Sidgwick, came in and was stealing part of her hour from her, she fetched a large sheet of white paper and a very black pencil and, lying down on the hearth-rug, wrote in capitals (the only letters she had mastered at that time) WEN WILL HE GO ? Of course he saw this, and with much laughter all round, at any rate from three of us, cut his visit short. Another time, at the end of this special hour of hers, her nurse came for her, and she was running off when I said, " Oh, Philippa, you are forgetting your doll." She looked very grave, and, holding up her little hand, said, " Ssh, don't call her a doll. I don't want her to know she's a doll." It would be interesting to know if such consideration for the feelings of a doll is frequently shown by children. I very much enjoyed teaching her myself at the very beginning of her baby lessons. It was intensely interesting, and I had received some useful hints from my friend Mrs. R. W. Dale, wife of the well-known Birmingham scholar and divine. Mrs. Dale was a connection by marriage of the Fawcett family at Salisbury, and a very staunch and dear friend to me.

When Philippa was a little girl we acquired a dog, a Dandie Dinmont, named Oddo, to whom we were all devoted. Philippa's affection to him was unbounded.

She said triumphantly, "Now, if people ask me if I have a brother I shall say yes." When she was about fifteen we thought we ought to take advantage of living for several months of each year in Cambridge to get her some really good mathematical teaching, and a Trinity Hall friend of my husband, Mr. G. B. Atkinson, undertook to give her short lessons once or twice a week. She used to bring work from him to do at home. No sooner had she finished it than she would dart out of the house to post it in a pillar-box about two hundred yards away. I inquired why she did this; it would reach Mr. Atkinson, I said, just as soon if it were posted at the regular time with the other letters. She replied, " I don't feel comfortable as long as it is in the house." I did not know whether this was a good or bad symptom, but it was not long before Mr. Atkinson told my husband that barring accidents he considered it a certainty that she would be a High Wrangler. It is hardly necessary to mention here that in 1890, when she took her mathematical tripos she was above the Senior Wrangler, and that in 1891, when she took the second part of the tripos, she was in the first division of the first class. There were only two men so placed—Mr. Bennett, of St. John's, and Mr. Crawford, of King's. Mr. Bennett had been in the same mathematical classes as Philippa at University College, London, so those who taught them were quite prepared for their running neck and neck. Once, when I asked her how many were in her class at University College, she replied, " Two white boys, two black boys, and me."

One more little story of her must be told. After she had finished her tripos and was on the resident staff at Newnham College, she was calling one Sunday afternoon on Dr. and Mrs. H. A. Morgan. He was then Master of Jesus, and had been Sixth Wrangler in his time. He showed Philippa a mathematical puzzle which had been

going the rounds among his friends ; he had not succeeded in finding the solution of it, and he said to her,
" Don't break the Sabbath, Philippa, by working at it
to-day, but look at it to-morrow, and if you find the
answer send it to me on a post card." She did find it,
for she solved the problem in her head on her way back
to Newnham, so that the Master received it on a post
card the next morning. He was very pleased about
this, and told me about it the next time we met.

I felt too keenly about what I was almost certain was
going to happen when the tripos lists were read out
in the Senate House in 1890 to dare to be present. My
father was there with two young granddaughters, and
they described the scene to me. I also, of course, had
many letters about it. I was intensely rejoiced, my only
regret being that my husband was not here to share
my joy with me. I had literally hundreds of telegrams
of congratulation. They showered in upon me like
snowflakes in a storm. At last even the phlegmatic
reserve of the telegraph boy was overcome, and he
asked, " Whatever is going on in this house ? Is it a
wedding ? " Our dear old housekeeper, who was
answering the door, exclaimed, " Oh no ! a great
deal better than that."

I always consider myself a lucky person, and this
impression was confirmed by the result of Philippa's
tripos examination. I should have been overjoyed if
any girl, even the daughter of my dearest enemy, had
gained a similar distinction. But that this great honour
should come to our own child was a joy that could hardly
be expressed. I had been full of rejoicing when, three
years previously, Miss Agneta Ramsay, now Mrs.
Butler, had been placed in the first division of the first
class in the Classical Tripos at Cambridge, and that she
had occupied this position in solitary grandeur so that
Punch had been iustified in a good cartoon showing

PHILIPPA FAWCETT IN HER ROOM AT NEWNHAM COLLEGE,
CAMBRIDGE, 1891.

From a photograph.

To face page 140.

a first-class carriage and the guard turning back all masculine aspirants with the words " For ladies only." The distinguished position of two women students, the one in Classics and the other in Mathematics, was such a triumphant answer to all the sneers and jeers showered upon the Women's University Education movement in former times. Philippa's coach, Mr. Hobson, told me on the authority of the examiners that it had been a strong year, and that she was 400 marks (or 13 per cent.) ahead of the senior. I heard from Dr. Montagu Butler, the Master of Trinity, who, in the course of a very kind letter, said, " I only wish you could have seen your dear daughter in the Senate House at the moment of her triumph. You could not have seen a more perfect picture of modest maidenly simplicity. This can be no surprise to you or to any who have known her. Still, the picture presented was singularly impressive and touching." Another charming letter was from our old friend Mr. E. A. Beck, afterwards Master of Trinity Hall. He wrote to congratulate us both upon the brilliant success of Philippa, " on which this college with one accord looks with an interest and a strong family feeling which you can well understand." Another letter gave me details gathered from her examiners of the character of her success. One of these contains the following passage : " She was ahead on all the papers except two, so that the examiners were sure that her place had no element of accident in it, but that in any similar examination she would have accomplished the same feat. Her work was similar to that of her father (but with greater mathematical know-ledge), no shots, no sheets of paper wasted, but grasp of question and proper application, the only errors and erasures being unimportant ones of analysis, and these only occasional." A telegram from Miss Emily Davies was characteristic : " Magnificent news, almost overwhelming." Anna Bateson wrote : " I cannot imagine a more delightful thing having happened. It is splendid that it should be someone from Newnham, but that it should be Philippa makes it doubly so, and I am sure everyone will be as glad for you as for her. . . . They (the people in the neighbourhood, Ammonford, South Wales) all say now, 'Why don't they give women degrees?' to which I find it impossible to give any satisfactory reply." Then there was a very affectionate note from Evelyn, Lady Portsmouth, whom I greatly loved ; she wrote ; " Philippa's success gives me a slight delirium of joy. I congratulate you, and in so doing think of one who is gone, who would have been made so proud and happy could he have seen this now." Another dear woman friend wrote : " I just sat down and cried for joy." Letters came also from Miss Emily Lawless, Miss Cons, Mrs. Arthur Lyttelton, Miss Frances Power Cobbe, Lord Spencer, Mr. Frederick Harrison, Professor Adams (the Cambridge astronomer) and his wife ; even Sir Henry James (afterwards Lord James of Hereford) and Sir William Harcourt, both staunch enemies to the political side of the women's movement, wrote charming letters. Sir Henry James said that Philippa's achievement had considerably weakened his opposition to our political claims. This was, however, only a passing phase of emotionalism, and he soon returned to normal. Lord Courtney's letter was brief, and may be quoted almost in full :

DEAR MRS. FAWCETT,
    Magnificent !
    I was out at breakfast, and when I came in my wife told me the news. . . . I have always said it was cruel as well as foolish to predict great things beforehand, but Philippa has justified everything.
    Magnificent for her, for you, for all women.
                    Ever yours,
                    LEONARD COURTNEY.

My father had come from Aldeburgh bringing with

him two of his granddaughters, Marion and Christina Cowell, so that they might be in the Senate House when Philippa's position in the tripos was declared. I think they had probably heard from Philip Cowell, the brother of the two girls, then a scholar of Trinity, what was anticipated. He was Senior Wrangler two years later ; it made my father very proud that he had a granddaughter and a grandson of such outstanding capacity. In Philippa's year my people at Aldeburgh had evidently been told that they would hear and see something they would like if they came up. My father accordingly came, as I have said, accompanied by two granddaughters and took lodgings in Jesus Lane. Marion, always a graphic letter-writer, sent the following account to her mother :

It was a most exciting scene in the Senate this morning. Christina and I got seats in the gallery, and Grandpapa remained below. The gallery was crowded with girls and a few men, and the floor of the building was thronged by undergraduates as tightly packed as they could be. The lists were read from the gallery and we heard splendidly. All the men's names were read first, the Senior Wrangler was much cheered. There was a good deal of shouting and cheering throughout ; at last the man who had been reading shouted " Women." The undergraduates yelled " Ladies," and for some minutes there was a great uproar. A fearfully agitating moment for Philippa it must have been ; the examiner, of course, could not attempt to read the names until there was a lull. Again and again he raised his cap, but would not say " ladies " instead of " women," and quite right, I think. He signalled with his hand for the men to keep quiet, but he had to wait some time. At last he read Philippa's name, and announced that she was "above the Senior Wrangler." There was a great and prolonged cheering ; many of the men turned towards Philippa, who was sitting in the gallery with Miss Clough, and waved their hats. When the examiner went on with the other names there were cries of " Read Miss Fawcett's name again," but no attention was paid to this. I don't think any other women's names were heard, for the men were making such a tremendous noise ; the examiner shouted the other names, but I could not even detect his voice in the noise. We made our way round to Philippa to congratulate her, and then I went over to Grandpapa. Miss Gladstone was with him. She was, of course, tremendously delighted. A great many people were there to cheer and congratulate Philippa when she came down into the hall. The Master of Trinity and Mrs. Butler went up into the gallery to speak to her. Grandpapa was standing at the bottom of the stairs waiting for Philippa. He was a good bit upset. I entreated him not to upset Philippa, and he said he wouldn't. He pressed something into her hand—a cheque, I fancy. [It was really a ring.] She was very composed. A great many of the Dons came to shake hands with her. The undergraduates made way for her to pass through the hall and then they all followed her, cheering, and I saw her no more. Grandpapa called the servant girl of our lodgings up as soon as we got in, gave her ten shillings, telling her first that his granddaughter was Senior Wrangler. He said, " You are landlady's daughter, aren't you ? " She, not wishing to lose the ten shillings, and yet wishing to keep to the truth as far as possible, said, "Not quite." He replied, " Very nearly," and gave her the tip. Grandpapa is now lying down.

Lovingly yours,
MARION.

The Miss Gladstone mentioned in the foregoing letter was Helen, the third daughter of the statesman. She was for several years one of the Vice-Principals of Newnham College, and the Head of one of the Halls, and was a very strong and good social influence among all the students. Her thoughtful kindness in seeking out my father as described in the letter is thoroughly characteristic of her. I went down to Cambridge in the early afternoon of the great day, and witnessed the rejoicing among the students in the garden of Newnham the same evening. There were fireworks and a bonfire, and all the time-honoured machinery of a festival, except the letting off of firearms. An American friend of mine expressed her views on this subject : she said, " I wonder why men do not find out some better way of showing they are pleased than by making the same noises which they make when they are killing each other." Mary Bateson, a Newnham student, who was as distinguished in history as Philippa was in mathematics, led the revels, and to everyone's amusement the gay throng in the garden was presently joined by a body of young men from the neighbouring Selwyn College. They were all very charming, well-behaved boys, but the head parlourmaid from Newnham, who had almost the personality of a female butler, considered that the situation ought to be commanded by her critical eye, and sent a message to the Principal, Miss Clough, not to be alarmed, " I am here." No one had been either alarmed or had thought of alarm, and to round off the whole joyful occasion the motto on our Shakespeare calendar for the next day was appropriately :

> The Heavens hold firm
> The walls of thy dear honour : keep unshaked
> That temple, thy fair mind.

After our return to London, Philippa and I were invited to a garden party at Devonshire House. Lord Hartington was then Chancellor of Cambridge University. He stood looking melancholy and bored receiving the long file of guests and shaking hands with each ; somehow, as my daughter and I approached him, another girl slipped between myself and her, so that when it became our turn to be shaken by the hand by Lord Hartington, he said solemnly, " I congratulate you, Miss Fawcett," to the wrong girl. Philippa's comment on this was characteristic. " I gave a hasty glance at her and thought she was better for the cause than I was, though not quite all one could have wished, so it was better as it was."

Chapter XVI

GROWING ABSORPTION IN SUFFRAGE WORK

E VEN WHEN I was in the full rush of Suffrage work at home there were many things that made it very pleasant : the work itself often brought me into contact with interesting and charming people whom I should not otherwise have known. Dr. Martineau was one of these. We were preparing a booklet giving opinions favourable to our movement from Leaders of Religious Thought : we had telling passages from Dr. Temple, Bishop of London and afterwards Archbishop of Canterbury, the Rev. F. D. Maurice, the Rev. J. Llewellyn Davis, the Rev. R. W. Dale of Birmingham, Dr. Clifford, and many others ; we wanted to be able to add some expression favourable to our aim from Dr. Martineau. He was then our near neighbour, living in Gordon Square, and I was familiar with his beautiful head, as I had frequently seen him with his daughter at the Saturday Popular Concerts, but I had never been introduced to him. However, I wrote explaining my object, and asked leave to call, which was most courteously granted. I had a deeply interesting interview with him, and he was good enough to write something for us, expressing his sympathy with our movement. This was not very long before his death in 1900. I was thankful to be able to carry away with me for the rest of my life a vivid recollection of his noble and beautiful personality.

MILLICENT GARRETT FAWCETT

From a photograph taken about 1892

To face page 146.

Sometimes calls were made upon me of an unusual nature. The then Lord Denman, the second Baron, appeared one day at my house. He had lately, and as we thought with more zeal than discretion, introduced a Women's Suffrage Bill in the House of Lords. Possibly he had heard that we had not smiled on his efforts on our behalf ; anyway he came to explain and expound his own point of view. He said, " My object is that my then widow should have a vote." I liked him for this, which was rather different from the way many men regard their " then " widows. He went on to talk on general politics. Of one thing he was quite assured, and that was that Mr. Balfour was not the man to lead the Conservative Party. I naturally inquired, " Why ? " and he at once rejoined, " He says he don't take any pleasure in killin' things." A rather curious reason, I thought, for considering a man disqualified to lead a great party. Sometimes callers were of an equally unexpected and delightful character. I was sitting at home, rather tired and rather cross, after a long exhausting committee. A new little maid, named Martha, came in and said, "A lady to see you, m'm. She won't give her name, but she wants to see you on business." " Now, Martha," I replied, " that is what beggars always say. You must learn to know when people are beggars, and not let them in." Then I went downstairs and found the supposed beggar standing on the doormat. I saw at once that she was a lady, and asked her in, and was, I hope, welcoming to her before she spoke. Her first words were, " I have brought you £1,000 to use in any branch of your Suffrage work which you may think most needs it." She gave me her name, but said I must not make it known. The generous gift was, she assured me, not from herself, but from a friend whose name she was not allowed to reveal. Imagine my joy. It was the first time that such a magnificent gift had been made to our cause, and its unexpected arrival made it all the more welcome. I am glad to say that immediately the front door had been shut upon this ministering angel my first thought was at once to find Martha. " Martha, Martha ! " I cried, " it was not a beggar, it was a lady who brought us a thousand pounds for our work." Even now these delightful things happen from time to time. On 1st October 1923 I had £1,000 brought to me for the N.U.S.E.C. in the same totally unexpected way, and in November of the same year another thousand pounds for our London Society for Women's Service, from an entirely different source. I look upon these wonderful events as just my luck, and I began to expect £1,000 once a month. This expectation has not, however, been fulfilled.

Chapter XVII

THE SOUTH AFRICAN WAR AND THE CON-CENTRATION CAMPS COMMISSION

THE EVEN TENOR of our work at home for the enfranchisement of women was dramatically interrupted from 1899 to 1902 by the South African War. I cannot say " suddenly " interrupted, because war had been threatening some time before it actually began. It was declared by the Boers on Dingaan's Day, 16th December 1899, and within a few days they were besieging three British towns, Mafeking, Kimberley, and Ladysmith.

The war naturally caused an almost complete suspension of work for Women's Suffrage. But the actual origin and cause of the war were on lines that very strongly emphasized the reasonable and irrefutable nature of the claim of British women to a share in the government of their country. For in the first instance the war in South Africa was caused by President Kruger's persistent refusal to admit Englishmen and other " Uitlanders " long settled in the Transvaal to any share in its citizenship. They and their industries were heavily taxed ; a very large proportion of the whole revenue of the State was derived from them, but they were denied the vote and therefore had no share in controlling the expenditure or the policy of the State in which they lived. They not unnaturally raised the cry, " No taxation without representation," and in other respects almost inevitably took up and repeated the arguments and protests which for many years we had urged on behalf of the unenfranchised women of Great Britain. Of course these causes of the war were by no means universally accepted as correct, and there was a great deal of force in the arguments of those who held that it was the disastrous Jameson Raid in 1895 which made the war a certainty. But those who most confidently took this view, generally failed to ask themselves, " What caused the Jameson Raid ? " Looking back on the whole situation with our knowledge of recent events, I believe it is possible to say with some confidence that if the machinery set up by the League of Nations had existed at the close of the nineteenth century, the South African War could have been easily prevented. The brief sketch which I have given of the events which led up to the war fairly represents, I think, the opinion of the great majority in this country upon them. But there was not a united nation to meet the war in 1899 as there was to meet the war of 1914. On the contrary, the nation was bitterly divided, and the subject became one of fierce party controversy. This only added to the streams of argument and oratory, and as these went on they continually emphasized the traditional British belief in self-government based on a wide extension of the franchise. In the Press the strongest opponents of the enfranchisement of British women in Great Britain were among the loudest in denouncing the disfranchisement of British men in South Africa. The *Spectator*, for instance, at that time a fanatical opponent of political liberty for women, dwelt eagerly and with much force on the value and significance of the vote. " We dwell so strongly on the franchise," it declared, " because it includes all other rights, and is the one essential thing." This is exactly what we had been saying for years, and what we considered we had proved ; we therefore found that, although during the war Suffrage propaganda at home had been to a large extent suspended, our old enemies were doing our propaganda for us and using arguments which we could transfer without the change even of a comma to our own case. The speeches of our opponents gave us examples of this, and we were continually looking them up and filing them. Therefore our movement went on growing, all the better, perhaps, because of our silence, in an atmosphere in which a deeper sense of the value of citizenship had come into being.

It will be remembered that after a disastrous opening for the British in December 1899, Lord Roberts was sent out to South Africa as Commander-in-Chief of the British Forces, with Lord Kitchener as his second in command. Rumour said that these appointments were due to the initiative of Queen Victoria. They arrived early in January 1900, and our military position immediately showed a vast improvement. In rapid succession the sieges of Kimberley and Ladysmith were raised. The Boer General, Cronje, with an army of 5,000 men, surrendered at Paardeberg, in the Orange Free State, on 27th February, and Lord Roberts entered Bloemfontein on 13th March. Mafeking was relieved on 17th May, and an advance was made to Pretoria, which was occupied on 5th June. I remember a young subaltern's letter, describing what he saw on the occasion of Cronje's surrender at Paardeberg. One sentence of it ran thus : " There sat Cronje, wolfing into our ham." I think, therefore, it may be inferred that Cronje and his 5,000 men surrendered to hunger, and that the victors were not very lavishly supplied with food. Everything that the armies, whether Boer or British, and everything that the civil population needed, except on the sea-coast, had to be brought to them on a single line of railway. This was a controlling element in the situation, as we had frequent opportunities of observing.

But the successes just mentioned, although they rendered the ultimate victory of the British a certainty, did not stop the war. Guerilla fighting went on over large areas of the sparsely inhabited country. The back veldt, as it was called, had possibly never even heard of the British victories. Lord Kitchener, who had succeeded Lord Roberts as Commander-in-Chief, determined, as a means of bringing the war to an end, that the country should be cleared of its inhabitants, and these were brought into what were known as concentration camps. This policy was carried out, all the inhabitants of the regions dealt with, British as well as Boer, being brought into these camps, and blockhouses for British troops were placed on all the railways and other routes. The time of year when this was being carried out was in the South African winter, a very warm winter we should consider it in comparison to ours, but none the less treacherous on account of the great variation between night and day temperatures. In the middle of the day the sun had great power, while at night there was often frost enough to cover shallow pools with ice and stop the flow of water in pipes and taps. A severe epidemic of measles followed by pneumonia broke out in the concentration camps, and there was a terribly high mortality, especially among the young children. The Boer women and children had often been with their menfolk on commando, and reached the camps badly run down by over-fatigue and unsuitable food. These were particularly a prey to disease of various kinds.

Party feeling was running very high at home, and everyone concerned with the administration of the camps was spoken of by their political opponents as if they were Herods presiding and gloating over a deliberately planned massacre of the innocents. The Government ardently desired to check or prevent the great mortality in the camps, and the question arose as to how to do it. All this was very much occupying people's minds, when one day, in mid-July 1901, Mrs. Alfred Lyttelton came in to see me, and asked me if I should be willing to go to South Africa, starting almost immediately and accompanied by other ladies with expert knowledge of infant welfare, to make recommendations to the Government with the view of improving the conditions, especially of child-life in the camps. Mrs. Lyttelton's husband, Alfred Lyttelton, was then a member of the Government. He was admired, beloved and trusted by all parties and all sections of the country as few men have ever been, and although his wife did not say so, I felt sure she came, in a sense, as a messenger from him and the Government. I at once consented to go, and told Mrs. Lyttelton I could be ready to start in a week or less. My colleagues were to be Lady Knox, wife of General Sir William Knox, then on active service in South Africa, Miss Lucy Deane, a trained Inspector of Factories and also an expert in Infant Welfare work. We were to be six altogether ; the other three were already in South Africa. Two of these were medical women, Dr. Jane Waterston of Cape Town, and Dr. Ella Scarlett ; the third was a trained nurse, formerly a Sister in Guy's Hospital, Miss Katherine Brereton. I did not know any of my colleagues except by hearsay. Those of us who were in England were given berths on a troopship ; I was accompanied by my daughter, Miss Deane by her sister, and Lady Knox by a maid. We soon became friends, and sat on deck discussing plans and learning a smattering of Taal, so that we should be able at least to interchange a few words with the inhabitants of the camps. There was a Cape Dutch nurse on board who superintended our studies in the Taal and helped us about pronunciation. She also produced little books of poems in Taal, all of which were

translations from the English, such as, " We are Seven,"
" Lucy Gray," and Southey's verses about little Peterkin
and Wilhelmine. We inquired about literature in the
Taal which was not a translation, but our teacher did not
seem to see what we were driving at, so at last we had
to put it to her rather bluntly, " Is there nothing of
your own ? No verses or books to read written originally
in your own language ?" Then she at once replied,
" Yes, there is plenty, there is *Tit-Bits*." After this we
gave up trying to make our teacher understand what
we wanted. As we approached Cape Town, one of the
most beautiful and impressive views it is possible to
imagine broke upon us, with the noble Table Mountain
for a magnificent background ; but our hearts nearly
stood still when we saw all the flags at half-mast. We
had been nearly three weeks at sea ; of course there was
no " wireless " in those days, and we dreaded to hear
of some new calamity. Queen Victoria had died in the
preceding January and I had lost a very dear niece
just before I left England, and now Death, it seemed,
had laid his hand on us again, and we were all asking
in our hearts, " Who is it ?" The first boat which
reached the ship brought us the answer to our question
and told us of the death of the Empress Frederick.
Life had brought her so many sorrows and such anguish
of disappointment that we felt Death must have come
to her as a friend. The great lines arose in our minds :

> O let him pass ! He hates him
> That would upon the rack of this rough world
> Stretch him out longer.

I should like to say something about our principal
colleague in our work of the inspection of the concentration camps.

Dr. Jane Waterston was, and is, a very remarkable
woman, an outstanding personality in the whole of South

Africa. She had originally come out to the Eastern Province as a medical missionary, attached to the great establishment founded by Dr. Stewart and others at Lovedale. She worked there for years before she settled in private practice in Cape Town. She was an ardent defender of the rights of the native races of Africa, but full of common sense and practical wisdom upon this and other subjects. It was a joy to walk down Adderley Street, Cape Town, and watch the glow of ardent affection and reverence which lighted up the dark faces of almost every native we met as they recognized her. She was an indefatigable medical visitor at Robin Island, the Leper Settlement near Cape Town. Her male colleagues wrote and spoke enthusiastically of her professional work, but rather annoyed me by referring to her as the best man among them ! It is so difficult for most men to understand that it is a very left-handed compliment to a woman to say when she shows intelligence or force of character that she might be a man. That is one of the things, however, which we have almost got through and have come out on the other side. Throughout our camp work all the most difficult and fatiguing jobs were voluntarily undertaken by our dear Dr. Jane. Such things as the source of water supply to be investigated, involving a tramp of a mile or more over the veldt ; slaughter places, drainage and sanitation to be inspected—these were the jobs which Dr. Jane claimed as hers by divine right. Her knowledge and experience of the country were an enormous advantage to us. She was a great politician and an out-and-out Britisher by instinct and training ; but in the presence of a sick child or woman she was nothing but the skilled and tender physician sparing no pains or cost to restore the invalid to health.

We found Cape Town riven into hostile sections, full of gossip, of inventions and unfounded suspicions

and fears.   We were conducted to the Mount Nelson
Hotel, and had not been there many hours before an
A.D.C. from Government House arrived.   He was
an extremely polite young man, but he had to deliver
a not at all polite message, namely, that His Excellency
and Lady Hely Hutchinson would prefer us not to call
at Government House.   It was a little perturbing,
for it was our first experience of being desired not to call
on the great and mighty, but we guessed it was a symptom
of the rages and feuds which were then tearing the social
world in Cape Town into violently hostile factions.
We discovered then, and later, that in a war the people
who have not fought are much more fierce and vindictive
than those who have.   We sought and obtained an
interview with a committee of ladies in Cape Town
who were ardently in sympathy with the Boers.   We told
them that we had at our disposal a moderate sum of
money from private sources which we wanted to spend
in a manner most calculated to be of service to the people
in the camps : could they, with their experience, tell us
how best it could be employed ?   They immediately
replied, " Send them calico to wrap their corpses in."
This startled us.   We had while on the ship prepared
a list of twenty-one questions bearing on what is now
called Welfare Work, but we had never thought of this.
Our twenty-one questions dealt with water supply,
sanitation, kitchens, hospitals, occupations, education,
the care of orphans, and so on.   We now added a twenty-
second, dealing with the reverent treatment of the dead,
including the provision of clean and orderly mortuaries
and cemeteries, and suitable coffins and shrouds.   In the
ensuing months we visited thirty-three camps, some of
them twice, and in each of them we made special inquiries
on these points, *and in not one single instance did we meet
with a vestige of complaint* from the people most nearly
concerned as to any failure on the part of the administra-

tion to observe the pious reverence for the dead which is instinctive in Dutch and British alike. It is almost unnecessary to say that we did not in this, nor in any other of our inquiries, content ourselves with asking questions solely of the officials. We did this as a matter of course, but we also went, either singly or two of us together, to visit the women in their tents and endeavoured by friendly talk to encourage them to tell us whatever was uppermost in their minds. We had many interesting conversations in this way, and never once did a single human being utter a word which justified the Cape Town ladies' insinuation that what these poor people wanted most was calico to wrap their corpses in. They naturally wanted a great many things, but not this.

But the Cape Town Ladies' Committee had made another suggestion to us, namely, that we should bring into the camps a supply of candles and distribute them among the Boer women. I shall never forget the lugubrious severity with which one of them said to us, " It is very difficult to nurse an invalid by the light of a match." This also was a grievance of which we did not hear in the camps. We did hear, however, that the Boer women were very expert in using candles as a means of signalling to their friends on commando in the quiet hours of the night. I for one could not blame them if they did ; if we had been in their position, should we not have done the same thing ? The instinct of the non-combatant to help the combatant on his own side is very powerful and practically universal. It was for doing this in 1915 that Edith Cavell laid down her life. But of course no Englishman ever dreamed of killing a Boer woman who helped or tried to help her own brethren in the field. The military administration did, however, refrain from giving them a plentiful supply of candles to do it with.

We left Cape Town in a special train supplied by the Cape Government. Each of us had what was apparently a second-class compartment fitted with sleeping accommodation. There was a large saloon for our meals, with a travelling kitchen attached, and we also had a Portuguese cook named Gomez, and the services of a young Tommy named Collins, lent to us by General Knox, Lady Knox's husband. We looked all round the arrangements made for our comfort and security with interest, curiosity, and gratitude, for these railway carriages were to be our home for about five months. A kind old gentleman, a Scot, the manager of the C. G. Railway, came to see that all his directions for our welfare had been observed, and to bid us farewell. We thanked him for having looked after us with so much forethought, but he remarked rather dourly that we should be glad enough to see the last of our railway home. As he knew there were to be six of us, he placed six copies of the latest " Railway Guide," quite useless though they were, on the table of the saloon. I smiled when I saw them, and said to him that I perceived that he thought we should very soon not be on speaking terms with each other. I assured him he was mistaken, and that we should get on very well. And so we did. Having plenty of work and a rational distribution of it amongst the members of our party was very soothing ; so was the possession by each of us of a small spot where we could be alone. I never quarrelled with any of my companions. Of course I did not like them all equally, but I think we were all equally eager to fulfil the work we had undertaken. Our last action together when our work was over was to attend the marriage of our youngest member—we used to call her our baby—the Hon. Ella Scarlett, M.D., to Lieut. Synge, whose acquaintance she had made before she joined us, when working at the camp at Norval's Pont. I knew something of Mr. Synge's family, his father having been a well-known clergyman in Ipswich, and at the wedding it was I who gave the bride away.

But now I must try to describe our work. Our full reports were, of course, sent home to the Government, and were published in a Blue Book, Cd. 893, in 1902. My own personal copy I interleaved with numerous photographs taken by my colleagues or myself or acquired by us from other amateurs.

The inhabitants of the camp were rationed free of cost to themselves with ample supplies of meal, meat, coffee, sugar, salt, and condensed milk, proportioned in quantity to the number of the family. In Natal potatoes, and sometimes fresh vegetables, were added, and later, on our recommendation, a supply of rice was given in all the camps. I give a copy of a Transvaal ration ticket for one week : the total number in the family was five, three adults and two children, one under five. They received every week : 3½ lb. of flour, 3½ lb. of sugar, 1½ lb. of coffee, 1 lb. of salt, 4 lb. of rice, 13 lb. of meat, 1 bar of soap, 1 bottle of milk for the baby. If the meat were lean, ¾ oz. of dripping or fat bacon was substituted for an equal weight of meat daily. Besides these necessaries of life, the administration of the camps supplied clothing, including boots, full medical attendance and nursing, also education and religious services, conducted by the various ministers in their own language. It was not an easy matter to get really competent and kindly men to act as superintendents of the camps. We found one or two really grossly incompetent men in charge and recommended their removal, but we did not come across one single instance of cruelty or even of harshness. Able-bodied and active men had naturally joined the Army and were fighting, while men who were not able-bodied had gone to Europe or down to the Coast towns. The occupants of the camps were in many cases extremely " slim," to use the Boer word, meaning " artful." They would apply to the Superintendent for clothing, dresses, stockings, etc., and he would go on supplying these until his suspicions had been aroused, when a search party would visit the tent of the delinquent to find, perhaps, half a dozen dress lengths, besides piles of various kinds of underclothing. Trickery of this kind was kept in check in the best organized camps by means of a " Camp Committee " consisting of the leading Boer men and women in the place. The old-fashioned Boer gentleman or lady has very courtly, gracious manners, and always addressed us as friends who were desirous of helping them. From one of these " Camp Committees " a complaint reached us that the ration of fuel allowed per head was inadequate. We immediately arranged to meet the Committee and go into the whole question with them. We pointed out that although the daily supply of fuel per head was very small, it was exactly the same as that served out to our soldiers in the field, and that they managed to make it enough by clubbing together and having a mess, say, for a dozen or more. The leader of the Committee replied, " Honoured ladies, what you say is very true, but we Boer people could not do it ; we should all have to be born again and a new love would have to be created among us ; each one of us must boil his own pot." And then a Boer lady put in her word, and said, " Yes, and if I put a fat piece in, I like to take a fat piece out." Plenty of medical comforts, they said, including candles, had been issued during the epidemic. We told them that the doctor had informed us of an enteric case brought into the hospital only the day before, in the twentieth day of the disease. They were much concerned, and felt this touched their efficiency as a committee charged with looking after the health of the camp. They admitted that there was a great tendency to conceal sickness, and also admitted the prevalence of imposture as regards the supply of clothing. We told them that at home in London cases of imposture were very frequent when relief was being distributed, and possibly they had found the same. They replied, " By hundreds." The chief need at that moment, they told us, was for boots. There were twelve shoemakers in the camp who could make fifty pairs a week if they could get the leather. We promised to speak about this. In conclusion, the leader of the Committee said to us, " Ladies, we wish to speak with thankfulness of the kindness and goodness of our Superintendent from the beginning of the camp and all along. Everything he could do for us he has done." This good man, Capt. Gostling, died not very long after our visit, of septic pneumonia, caught from the children in the hospital. His funeral was attended by a great concourse of the camp people, who said of him, " He has been a father to us." In another camp not far removed we found also an efficient Camp Committee, in this case consisting of thirty ladies. On our arrival they asked to see us, and, of course, we gladly agreed. The meeting was interesting, for they were all willing to talk for the most part reasonably and to the point. Towards the end, however, they became at variance with one another, especially on the subject of the Dutch matron, whom some of them distrusted. Several of them said, " We want the English to distribute things," and the same thing was repeated to us by some of the principal men in the camp, who said, " We would rather have an Englishman at the head of all the departments in the camp."

There was one woman who had been present, but rather silent, at our meeting with the Camp Committee ; when the others had departed she remained behind and said, " I am English ; my husband has never fought for the Boers. I only wish to say how thankful I should be to know that my two sisters, who are loyal refugees in the camp at Durban, are being as well treated as we are here."

For the most part we found the women in the camps gentle and friendly in their manners. In the camp at Harrismith I was calling on two Boer ladies, mother and daughter ; after preliminaries they told me that in their own home in a well-known village they had heard of the expected arrival of a considerable body of British troops, and they said, " We were terrified because we had heard dreadful things of them. Then they came and remained five months, and we did not, all that time, hear even one rough word from them." And they wound up their narrative by saying, "And now we will stick up for the British till we lie in our graves." Of course we did not always hear such pleasant things, and sometimes attempts were made to impose upon us by exhibiting strips of meat half converted into biltong, the sun-dried preparation the Boers use on commando, and pass it off to our ignorant eyes as the meat that had been served out to them as fresh that morning. Sometimes, too, Boer women would rush out upon us as we passed their tents and call out in their broken English, " De British not having been able to conquer de men, are now making war on de women and children." This we at once recognized as a quotation from party oratory imported from Great Britain. It did not make us angry ; but we rejoined that they too must have had experience in making war on Basutos, Zulus, or other natives, and when they had done so we had never heard that they had provided the womenfolk and other non-combatants among their enemies with food, clothing, and education, besides church services and hospital attendance. We found that nothing preserved our own equanimity so much as the constant endeavour to put ourselves in the place of the people we had come out from England to help. We had the pleasure in several places of coming across a party of Quaker ladies who had been sent out from home by the Society of Friends on very much the same mission as ourselves ; in one of them I discovered an old friend, Miss Hogg, of Dublin. Her party had come to much the same conclusions about the camps as we had, and they had cabled their committee at home to cease sending out cases of condensed milk, for instance, because everything of that sort was already being amply supplied by the Government authorities. Their committee chose not to believe them, and they were being pursued by huge packing-cases filled with the best brands of condensed milk. They took counsel with each other what they had better do with it, and came to the conclusion that to prevent waste and confusion it was best to hand it over to the Government authorities. General Sir John Maxwell was the head of the camps administration in the Transvaal. He learned their errand, and received them, of course, most courteously. He sat at his desk making out a formal receipt to be sent to the Friends' Committee in England, and as he handed it to the ladies he said, "And pray thank your committee for their handsome contribution to the cost of the war." Miss Hogg told us this, and was quite Irish enough to see the joke of it.

All through the camps we found almost without exception that the schools were a great success. There had been no attempt whatever by the Boer Government in the Transvaal to provide organized education for their people, and they availed themselves eagerly and in considerable numbers of the facilities for education which the camp schools afforded. It was rather touching to see grown-up young men and women sitting among the children and learning with them ; the most popular subjects with these adults were English and arithmetic. Dutch teachers were in many instances appointed in the schools. It interested us on one occasion to hear a Dutch schoolmaster instructing his class how to grapple with the pronunciation of the English G. He wrote on the blackboard the letters D, T, Z, and then ended with a half-suppressed sneeze, which he could not express by letters of the alphabet. We had never realized before that our poor English G presented such difficulties to foreigners, though we knew how curiously difficult the Dutch G was to us.

In this journey through the concentration camps I first came to know and value the extraordinary lovable qualities of the British Tommy. He was kindness and gentleness itself to every child and woman among the refugees ; he was also generous to a fault. He would give thoughtlessly and profusely to those he came across, and although he was a good grumbler on his own account when things were going smoothly, his spirits always seemed to rise when he was in acute discomfort and misery himself. I have seen our Tommies bivouacking in a station in the pouring rain, and have heard no grousing from them under what must have been physical misery. A lady with whom we made friends at De Aar told us of recent floods there owing to the rapid rising of the river after torrential rain. The men were ordered to save the forage supplies, and were working for hours up to their waists in water, shouting at the top of their voices some soldiers' chanty, such as, " Oh why did I leave my nice little 'ome in Bloomsberree ? Where for three and six a week I lived in Luxuree."

What we saw in the camps and especially the eagerness of the people in them to get education, led my daughter to apply to the Government at home for leave to go back and take part in the setting up of permanent educational machinery in the Transvaal, then under the control of Mr. E. B. Sargant, and later of Mr. (now General Sir) Fabian Ware. She returned to Newnham in 1901, but came out again in 1902 to share in the interesting work of establishing public elementary education in the Transvaal. I went to see her there in 1903, and revisited many of the places I had seen on my first visit, my dear friend Katherine Brereton bearing me company. On this second visit, the war being over, I saw something of the gradual recovery of the country from its devastating effects ; railway and other bridges were repaired, houses rebuilt ; animals, sheep, and oxen looking less like concertinas ; the horrid flocks of vultures had vanished and the great veldt was less thickly strewn with dead animals. But I also saw something of the crowd of orphans which every war leaves behind it. The new Transvaal Government had assembled many of these poor children at Irene, where they were under the care and guidance of a most gentle and kindly lady, Miss Frances Taylor, sister of Mrs. George Cadbury. She and I made the forty-eight hours' journey from Johannesburg to Cape Town together, and had the carriage to ourselves ; we therefore had many opportunities for conversation, of which we thoroughly availed ourselves. One thing which Miss Taylor said stuck in my memory. It was this : " Do tell my brother-in-law, Mr. George Cadbury, that the concentration camps were not in the least like what he imagined them to be." I replied by asking her if she had told him that herself. She said that she had, and I naturally rejoined, " If he did not believe you, what reason have I to hope that he will believe me ? "

On this second visit I was much interested in seeing something of the process of reconstruction going on to repair the ravages of the war : schools, orphanages, training colleges for nurses and teachers, all doing good work. At one place where a training college had been established I was particularly interested to find that the Dutch board of management had applied to a well-known institution in London to supply them with an English teacher of Domestic Economy. I hoped it looked as if the iron of hatred had not entered very deeply into their souls. My cousin Edmund, mentioned in an earlier chapter, had taken a very active part in the events which led up to the war ; but he never lost his appreciation of the fine qualities of the Boers. For one of the British and Boer cemeteries, I think at Wagon Hill, he wrote the following epitaph:

> Together, sundered once by blood and speech,
> Joined here in equal muster of the brave,
> Lie Boer and Briton, foes each worthy each.
> May Peace strike root into their common grave,
> And blossoming where the fathers fought and died,
> Bear fruit for sons that labour side by side.

To return to our first visit: we saw all the concentration camps except the one at Fort Elizabeth, of which even the pro-Boer ladies at Cape Town had no complaint to make ; some of the camps—for instance, Mafeking, Vryburg, and Kimberley—we saw twice, with a considerable interval between our two visits. We went back to Mafeking because of the renewal of a severe epidemic. On 15th August, just before our first visit, a number of Boer refugees had been brought in, and these had among them the following diseases : measles of a malignant type, enteric, malaria, fever, cerebro-spinal meningitis, whooping cough, and chicken-pox. The new-comers were neither examined nor isolated, and the various diseases which they had brought with them spread and flourished to an appalling degree. Our recommendations had been neglected, and therefore on our second visit we urged the removal of the Superintendent, and that adequate support should be given to Dr. Morrow, who was working loyally and faithfully to supply his place. We also put on record our opinion that the Superintendent and the former medical officer had been grossly to blame for the bad condition and the high death-rate in this camp. We felt more and more how great was the need of the people for fresh vegetables. "Bully beef and bread," we said in our report, "are

quite unsuitable diet for young children," and we urged
that if suitable food could not be provided for a camp
of 4,000 at Mafeking the camp should be removed
elsewhere. Lord Methuen, who was then in military
command of the district, did everything he could to help
the poor people in the camp, giving up to them his
own special E.P. tents to provide additional hospital
accommodation.

Our experience of our two visits to Kimberley was
instructive. On our first visit on 26th and 27th August
1901, we found two English ladies, Miss A. and Miss B.,
sent by a committee sitting in London. We called on
them ; it was quite easy to see which was their tent
because of the baths outside put upside down to dry.
We told them of our desire to see everything that we ought
to see in the camp and to make recommendations calculated to help the people and reduce the death-rate.
The deaths in August up to the 26th had been 141, of
which 93 had been of children of from 1 to 3 years.
We begged the ladies to put the knowledge they must
have acquired during their residence, so far as it was
possible, at our disposal ; but they were very uncommunicative, and obviously hostile to us. Miss A., who
had resided for five weeks in the camp, hardly told us
anything. She said she wished to remove to some other
camp "where the need was greater," and gave us no
practical suggestions of any kind. We thought the
death-rate just quoted showed as great a " need " as the
most zealous philanthropist could desire. We were
sorry they were so uncommunicative, because we felt
that if they had chosen to do so they could have helped
us very much. When we revisited the Kimberley camp
on 6th and 7th November we found the whole condition
immensely improved. The hospital accommodation
was adequate, the medical and nursing staff had been
reinforced ; four trained nurses, who were helped by

nine Boer probationers, were doing their work well. A camp matron who had been furnished by the Victoria League with four 10-gallon Soyer stoves was now looking after the convalescent children and supplying about 200 of them with a pint of good soup daily, and the excellent camp matron was just beginning to induce some of the Boer girls in the camp to act for her as visiting sisters. I believe she eventually got a staff of 12 of these girls. Miss A. and Miss B. were still in residence, but they had entirely changed in their demeanour towards us. From having been extremely cold and distant, they had become helpful and friendly ; and they told us frankly some of their recent experiences. Like ourselves they had been impressed by the great need in the camp of fresh vegetables, and had urged that practically the only way of getting them was to grow them on the spot. They had encouraged families to make little gardens of their own round their tents, offering prizes varying from £2 for an adult to 10s. for a child for the best garden ; but the supply thus promoted was inadequate. By co-operation with the authorities the Misses A. and B. had secured a promise of a grant of land in the immediate neighbourhood suitable for a large garden ; one of the ladies, on behalf of her committee in London, had promised £70 for fencing it in ; the Government promised water, an all-important and expensive item, besides seeds and implements, if the able-bodied men, of whom there were over 200 in the camp, would give the labour : these men called a meeting to consider whether they would do this or not, and they decided to refuse. Their line of argument was that the British had brought them there and were therefore responsible for providing them and the whole camp with everything that was necessary for their health. Both the ladies were very angry and disappointed. Our colleague, Dr. Jane Waterston, who had lived in Cape Colony for about half a century, was not at all surprised. It is one of the curses of having manual labour done by what most people consider an inferior race that labour itself is despised, the people who work being considered for that very reason inferior to those who overlook or do nothing. Miss B. said the people in the camp ought to be compelled to work, and told us, moreover, that in her opinion giving relief in the form of clothes did more harm than good ; both ladies had their doubts whether the gifts of clothing had not been taken down into the town of Kimberley and sold. Miss A. was also indignant at the alleged mal-administration at Cape Town in reference to £600 worth of goods sent out to her by her committee in London. Instead of forwarding them to her, the goods had been consigned to the Dutch clergyman resident in the camp, who had given them away without any reference to her or to the source from which they had been provided. We expressed sympathy, but did not feel we had any authority to take action in the matter.

We were decidedly pleased by the improvement which had taken place in the camp since our first visit. One woman with whom we had a good deal of conversation began rather bitterly that she did not know why she should be interned there, although her husband was on commando. She gradually became more friendly and said that she had nothing to complain of, that the food was good and sufficient, but that she would like the opportunity of earning a little pocket-money. Finally, looking round her tent, which was orderly and clean, she said, " It is beginning to be a little home to me."

We visited an orphanage in Kimberley of over 50 children, some of whom had been sent from the camp. Their ages varied from 1½ to 15 years. They looked healthy and were very bright and cheerful. They all spoke and understood English perfectly, and were learning their lessons, from Dutch teachers, out of English books.

When we were wending our way northwards again towards Pretoria, we sought an interview with General Kitchener. We had already had the advantage of several conversations with Sir A. Milner (now Lord Milner) and had told him our views about the necessity of a more varied dietary for the camps. He said he would support our application, but that the final decision must rest with Lord Kitchener, the allocation of extra trucks for the supply of the camps being a military matter. We therefore wrote and asked Lord Kitchener to see us. He agreed to do so, and sent his letter by General Sir John Maxwell, who had the camps especially under his charge. We had heard a good deal of Lord Kitchener's general opinion of the female sex, and rather smiled when we read his letter, for he expressed a wish that of the six of us only two should come on the deputation to see him. Our colleagues decided that these should be Lady Knox and myself. At the appointed hour General Maxwell arrived with a carriage to take us to Lord Kitchener's house. It was a charming and attractive building standing in a garden. We entered a large square hall, where we were asked to be seated while General Maxwell went into the room where Lord Kitchener was working. He left the door wide open, and we could not help hearing what he said. Again we smiled when we heard Lord Kitchener's voice inquire anxiously, " How many are there of them ? " In another minute we were shown into his room, and thereupon there ensued the most satisfactory and businesslike interview that I, at any rate, had ever had of an approximately similar nature. We set forth our views as to the necessity of providing greater variety in the dietary of the camps, and suggested the addition of rice to the rations on account of the number of ways in which, with even the simplest appliances, it could be cooked : stewed in milk for children, made appetizing for adults by adding a little curry powder, and so on.   He listened, and then said, " It is a question of trucks.   What you propose would mean an extra truck every week."   We said we had recognized that, but still urged that the extra truck should be provided.   He replied, " I allow 30 trucks per week for the food supply of the whole civil population of the Free State ; of these 30, 16 go to the camps and 14 to the rest of the civil population.   Do you wish me to give 17 to the camps and only 13 to the other civilians ? "   We exclaimed, " Certainly not.   We have been in these people's houses and know that already they are on very short commons before the end of each week.   We don't want to take an ounce from them ; we want an extra truck."   And an extra truck was agreed to, so that we felt that our talk with the great man had been very satisfactory.   Not an unnecessary word had been spoken, and therefore no time had been wasted. I liked him far better than any of the politicians I had gone to on deputations in London.   I always say that Lady Knox and I, after this interview with Lord Kitchener, received the compliment of our lives, for, after sampling two of us, he invited the whole six of us to dinner !   We did not all go ; but I think there were four of us.   Lord Kitchener took me in to dinner and I had much interesting conversation with him.   Later we had many talks about him with men of his staff and others.   We were told that on his journeys up and down the line or on horseback his keen eye saw everything and everybody, noting which men were doing their work well and which were slack or indifferent ; the first were promoted, the latter were, in the phrase of the day, " Stellenbosched," i.e. sent where they could do no harm.   Previous to our conversation with Lord Kitchener, we had had experience of subordinate officials of the type which believed that as soon as a thing was written down on a piece of paper, it was done.   One man had read out to us a list of groceries and asked us if we did not think it admirable English: another, when we emphasized the urgency of the fuel question, replied that he had indented for further supplies six weeks ago, and seemed quite hurt when we said that it had not actually arrived. These were the sort of people who ought to be " Stellenbosched," especially in a life-and-death business like war.

As soon as our work of inspection was over we repaired to Durban to draw up our final report. We stayed there over a week and worked daily at our report. It was signed by the whole six of us without reservations. The rest and excellent food of our good hotel were very welcome to us. We took a German ship, the *Herzog*, from Durban to Naples, and had a most interesting journey, putting in at Beira, Mozambique, Zanzibar, Dar-es-Salaam, Lamu, Aden, etc. At Lamu our ship was visited by a health officer, who turned out to be Dr. Alfred Paget, son of our old friend Sir George Paget, of Cambridge. He knew the place well, and was very good to us in helping us to see some of its curious manners and customs. A well-born native lady at Lamu is not content with being veiled ; when she walks abroad she is enclosed in a little movable tent, which is carried by a female attendant who precedes her mistress. I got a " snap " of this example of female modesty, but Dr. Paget was very careful not to allow this to be discovered. Our ship proceeded very leisurely up the East Coast of Africa. Zanzibar, we found a most entrancing place ; the architecture was very attractive, the immensely thick walls giving deep recesses to all windows and doors, and making an admirable effect. What I most remember of Zanzibar, however, is the wonderful beauty of the gold mohur-tree : it was in full blossom when we were there. The tree itself is as big as an English forest tree, and it was crowned by great trusses of scarlet flowers, glowing like fire against the dark blue sky. Sir Harry Johnston made a beautiful drawing of it, and used it as a sort of wall-paper design for a lining to one of his books on Africa. It was worth going to Africa just to see it in all its glory. We were also taken to Sir John Kirk's garden, a few miles out of Durban, full of all· kinds of botanical treasures. The frangipani-tree is what I best remember there : very lovely and very sweet-scented, but not equal to the gold mohur-tree.

There was a Boer lady on board the *Herzog* with whom we made friends. She told us that at the same time as the terrible infant mortality was raging in the concentration camps Mrs. Kruger, whom she knew intimately, had had six of her grandchildren to stay with her. The virulent form of measles which had swept the camps carried away four of these children in their grandmother's house, notwithstanding all the care which they received from the outset of the illness.

After we had returned home, and when our report had appeared as a Blue Book and had been circulated to both Houses of Parliament, I received the following letter from Mr. Brodrick, now Lord Midleton :

DEAR MRS. FAWCETT,
    Now that with the publication of the Blue Book your task may be said to be at an end, I cannot let time pass without expressing to you,. and your colleagues, who worked with you on the Concentration Camps Commission, my very sincere thanks for the able way in which you carried out the work which we asked you to undertake. The difficulties of it are well known to you who had to surmount them and did so with great success. The importance of it is patent to all who know what a great mass of questions were involved, and I hope you will kindly convey to your colleagues, both here and in South Africa, the thanks which are due to them and to yourself from me, on behalf of His Majesty's Government, for the very zealous and able way in which their arduous work was brought to a conclusion, which is, I think, universally recognized to have been satisfactory.

Yours very truly,
St. JOHN BRODRICK.

To this I replied :

Dear Mr. Brodrick,

Your kind letter received last night gave me very great pleasure, and I am sure my colleagues, both here and in South Africa, will be equally gratified by it. We also feel grateful for the kind and generous terms in which you and Mr. Chamberlain alluded to the work of our Commission, in the House of Commons, on Tuesday last. I am sure I may speak for my colleagues as well as for myself when I say it was a real satisfaction to us to be allowed to do some special work for our country in South Africa during the present crisis. I will not say that visiting and reporting on the camps was not fatiguing; but it was very interesting and quite straightforward and easy, for, as we said in reply to inquiries from the camp people at Aliwal North, all we had to do was " to see and hear all we could and to tell the truth."

Believe me, yours very truly,

Millicent G. Fawcett.

Chapter XVIII

THE LATER STAGES OF THE SUFFRAGE STRUGGLE. "MILITANCY"

THE NEW CENTURY had opened gloomily enough with the death of Queen Victoria and the prolongation of the South African War. These are things which everyone remembers, and they therefore call for no special record here. There was, however, one aspect of the deep national emotion caused by the death of the Queen which had a bearing on the progress of our work for the political enfranchisement of women. Universal homage was paid to the memory of the great Queen by leading statesmen of all parties and by the Press throughout the British Empire : it may be said throughout the world. The Queen was praised for her strong grasp and knowledge of public affairs, her devotion to duty, her sagacity, courage, and fidelity, and her good judgment in choosing her advisers : and comment was made on the fact that she combined all these fine political qualities with equal devotion to the duties of her domestic life. The very subjects which opponents of the enfranchisement of women had singled out in speech and writing as being beyond a woman's comprehension, such as National Defence and Foreign Politics, Queen Victoria had specially made her own, and in the Press mention was made of the deep impression her knowledge of them had made on foreign statesmen, such as Bismarck. We naturally pointed to this combination of qualities as a proof that the fears of the Anti-Suffragists were misplaced when they imagined that as soon as a woman got a vote she would throw to the winds her ordinary duties and occupations, neglect her home, and become a Mrs. Jellaby with no interests nearer than Borioboolagha.

We had made very great progress towards our goal and had secured a non-party majority in successive Parliaments ever since 1870 for the extension of the Parliamentary vote to women. We were still, however, faced by the implacable hostility of the majority of the Liberal leaders, and by the disconcerting levity with which Members of Parliament, when convenient, broke their pledges to us. It was in face of these facts that the Women's Social and Political Union was founded in Manchester by Mrs. Pankhurst, and her daughter, in 1903. They had been members of our Manchester Society of which Miss Esther Roper was secretary ; I think, also, Mrs. and Miss Pankhurst were at this time taking an active but, as it proved, only a temporary part in support of the Labour movement then just beginning to show its strength. Possibly the W.S.P.U. may have had in mind the old saying invented by one of the Irish Nationalists, " that it was useless to try to get any concessions for Ireland from a Minister of either party unless you approached him with a cow's tail in one hand and the head of a landlord in the other." However this may be, the Women's Social and Political Union soon conceived the idea that sensational methods were necessary before a substantial victory for Women's Suffrage could be won, but I did not hear, neither do I find in their writings, any trace of intentional violence or non-constitutional action at the beginning of their activity. At the outset they adopted the strictly orthodox and time-honoured method of asking questions of Ministers at public meetings. This, however, owing to the mishandling of the whole matter by the Liberal leaders and organizers, soon produced scenes of violence˗ and disorder. In October 1905, two years after the Women's Social and Political Union had been formed, the Conservative Party being then obviously on the brink of a heavy electoral defeat, a great Liberal demonstration was arranged in the Manchester Free Trade Hall, at which Sir Edward Grey, now Viscount Grey of Fallodon, was the principal speaker. Everything was organized with the view of emphasizing the note of victory : the organ pealed forth triumphant music, and the hall was filled to overflowing.

Miss Pankhurst and Miss Annie Kenny resolved to attend this meeting on behalf of the Social and Political Union, and to ask Sir Edward Grey the question, " Will the Liberal Government give votes to working women ? " As soon as they put this question an extraordinary hubbub arose : stewards tried to force the two girls down into their seats, shouts of " Sit down," " Be quiet," and other shouts of " Let the lady be heard," were bandied to and fro. The Chief Constable of Manchester came down from the platform and asked Miss Pankhurst and her friend to write out their question, and said he would himself take it to the platform and ensure its receiving a reply. To this they agreed, and they saw the Chief Constable return to the platform and hand it to Sir Edward Grey, who smiled and passed it on to the Chairman : it was then passed to every speaker in turn, but no attempt was made by Sir Edward Grey or anyone else to answer it. Why he omitted to answer a perfectly proper and legitimate political question has never been explained. He was a Suffragist himself ; the question, however, did not refer to his own views but to what the coming Liberal Government was going to do. The meeting became furious, and general uproar prevailed : the two girls were angry too, and shouted their loudest, while the stewards dragged them down with insult and violence.

Miss Pankhurst and Miss Kenny were flung out into the street, where they called an indignation meeting, and refused to disperse when called upon by the police to do so. In the meantime Sir Edward rose in the hall and said he was afraid that unwittingly he had been a contributing cause of the disturbance. He was, he said, himself in favour of Women's Suffrage, but he did not think it a fitting subject for that evening, as it was not a party question. This was by no means a satisfactory or a convincing reply. The sequel was that the two girls who had asked the question were brought up the next day at the police court, charged with assault and obstruction, and fined, the one ten shillings or seven days' imprisonment, and the other five shillings or three days. They both refused to pay the fines, and were at once hurried away to the cells. And this was in Manchester, almost on the site of the Peterloo franchise battle of 1819. To make the satire more complete, the Manchester Reform Club was, and I believe still is, decorated by a picture of the Peterloo massacre, " Dedicated to Henry Hunt, Esq., the chairman of the meeting, and to *the Female Reformers of Manchester* " who nearly 100 years earlier had been trampled down by the Cheshire Yeomanry Cavalry, for making a demand for votes for men.

Nothing could have been more inept than the official conduct of this whole episode. If Sir Edward had replied that the Liberal Government not being formed he could not say what it would do on the subject of women's votes, but that he himself was favourable to the inclusion of women in the next Reform Bill, no one could have complained, but to howl the questioners down and knock them about, then to charge them with obstruction and to fine them and, in default of payment, to imprison them, was a course more worthy of a Czardom than a free country. It put the whole question in a false position : the only thing that was some consolation was that the Press, which, with few exceptions, was very chary of admitting that there was any demand on the part of women for political freedom, now blazoned forth with tremendous energy the enormity of two young women rising in a public meeting to inquire of a Liberal leader what his party intended to do for the unenfranchised masses of women.

We had become quite accustomed to holding magnificent meetings in support of women's franchise with every evidence of public sympathy and support, and to receive from the Anti-Suffrage Press either no notice at all or only a small paragraph tucked away in an inconspicuous corner. The sensation caused by the action of the Women's Social and Political Union suddenly changed all this. Instead of the withering contempt of silence, the Anti-Suffrage papers came out day after day with columns of hysterical verbiage directed against our movement. At the outset the directors of these papers made the mistake of supposing that the Suffrage movement was capable of being killed by the batteries which were opened against it. If abuse and misrepresentation could have killed it, it most assuredly would have died in the early years of the twentieth century.

However, there were other things to fill the papers with, and it soon became evident that the Unionist majority obtained in the General Election of 1900 (402 Unionists to 263 Home Rulers) would not be maintained at the next General Election. Mr. Chamberlain was then conducting his raging, tearing campaign on behalf of Protection ; the by-elections were beginning to tell the tale which was to be confirmed by the General Election. This did not actually come until January 1906, and it resulted in one of the most smashing defeats ever suffered by the Conservative Party. The figures were : Unionists 157, Anti-Unionists 513. Everyone expected a Conservative defeat, but few had foreseen its extent.

From our point of view the most significant event of the General Election of 1906 was the birth of the Labour Party. Mr. Keir Hardie, its founder, and chairman of the Independent Labour Party, had been in Parliament for some years, and had appeared in the House as the first Labour Member. The election of 1900 had given him only a small group of colleagues of his own way of thinking ; but the election of 1906 greatly reinforced their numbers, and from that date the Labour Party in the House became a force to be reckoned with, and a force on our side in our Suffrage work. They were then forty-three in number, were independent of all other parties, had their own organization, their own Whips, and their own funds, and as a party they were definitely pledged to support the political equality of women. This fact gave us a new power and a new strength of which we soon began to feel the value. It is true that before this we had had three successive Conservative Prime Ministers favourable to our cause—Lord Beaconsfield, Lord Salisbury, and Mr. (now Lord) Balfour ; but they never had done anything substantial for us because of the opposition of the rank and file of their party. Mr. Bonar Law, who became Leader of the Conservative Party in 1911, was in the same position. He was quite in favour of votes for women, and had long been a member of the Glasgow Society affiliated to the N.U.W.S.S., but he told Miss Rathbone and myself, who came to see him on the subject, that the great bulk of his followers were opposed to us, and that he was not prepared to break up his party in an effort, and probably an unsuccessful effort, to help us.

In May 1906 the N.U.W.S.S. organized a big deputation, representing 26 organizations and numbering over 300 persons, to the new Prime Minister, Sir Henry

Campbell-Bannerman. He gave the deputation much the same reply, but from another angle, which we received from Mr. Bonar Law five years later. Sir Henry Campbell-Bannerman was personally favourable to our cause ; in fact, he said that the deputation had made out " a conclusive and irrefutable case," but that he could do nothing for us because of the opposition of other leaders of his own party. His last word of advice to the deputation was characteristic, and was long remembered and quoted. It was " *to go on pestering*." The W.S.P.U. were among the societies represented at the deputation, and they at once laid this advice to heart. Before the deputation withdrew Miss Kenny jumped on a chair and shouted out that she and those with whom she acted were not satisfied. After this, for several years, the whole country—indeed, one might almost say the whole world—rang with the doings of the Suffragettes, as the violent Suffragists came to be called. I would point out, however, that for the first five years of their existence, while they suffered extraordinary acts of physical violence, they used none, and all through, from beginning to end of their campaign, they took no life and shed no blood, either of man or beast. If there was great vehemence in their demonstrations, there was also great restraint. The whole body was perfectly under control. A very interesting and accurate account of the militant movement and the absolute discipline it maintained, reserving all power to Mrs. and Miss Pank-hurst, acting for a time in conjunction with Mr. and Mrs. Pethick Lawrence, but later quite independently, may be gathered from Miss May Sinclair's powerful novel, *The Tree of Heaven*. Some of the W.S.P.U. activities were original and amusing. I will quote one as an example : Public meetings and demonstrations are forbidden during the session within a mile of the Houses of Parliament. Watchful policemen are on guard to see that this regulation is observed, but they saw quite unperturbed the approach to Palace Yard of some half a dozen large pantechnicon vans : as soon as these reached the Cœur de Lion statue outside the House of Lords, they stopped, the doors flew open and out stepped from each van some ten or a dozen daintily clad Suffragettes, who immediately began to hold a meeting. All London, with the possible exception of the Home Office, was laughing over this little trick as soon as the incident became known.

It is difficult now to realize the tremendous sensation caused by the doings of the Suffragettes. Wherever one went nothing else was talked of ; intense hatred and contempt being frequently expressed and answered by equally vehement approval. An old friend of mine called out to me across the table at a dinner party that after the outrageous conduct of the militants he would never again do anything in support of Women's Suffrage. I retorted by asking him what he had done up to that moment, but got no answer.

A rather amusing instance of the degree to which Suffragist versus Suffragette occupied people's minds at this time may be gathered by quoting three advertisements which appeared in the " agony column " of *The Times* on the 7th, 10th, and 11th of February 1911, respectively :

7th Feb. Will the lady who at Dover Street Station on Wednesday afternoon gave up her seat to a lame gentleman, allow him to express his sincere thanks for a kindness from a woman, which is rare in this age of Suffragettes ?

10th Feb. Dover St. Tube. The lady who was happily able to assist a lame gentleman appreciates his thanks in *The Times* of the 7th inst., but must confess that she herself is an ardent advocate of, and worker for, Women's Suffrage.

11th Feb. I tender my humble apologies for a needless reflection on the courtesy of Women Suffragists in general and one in particular. In accepting this the lady will perhaps pardon an old man if he refuses to shed a lifelong prejudice as to the respective spheres of men and women.

At first, as I have said, and up to 1908, no physical
violence was used by the Suffragettes, though much
violence was used against them. On 23rd October
1906, Mrs. Cobden Sanderson, accompanied by a little
group of friends and sympathizers, went to the Central
Lobby of the House of Commons and there created
what was technically called "a disturbance"; i.e.
they waved flags bearing the words "Votes for Women"
and mounted the padded seats, from which they began
making speeches in support of the claim of women to
representation. She and three other women were
arrested and sentenced to two months' imprisonment
as ordinary offenders. Their whole object was to
demonstrate that women were no longer prepared to
wait patiently until some crumbs of citizenship should
be thrown to them from the rich man's table. Mrs.
Cobden Sanderson's more personal object was to prove
that working-class women were not going to be left
unsupported to bear the brunt of the agitation which the
W.S.P.U. had initiated. She and others had found that
the police were far more ready to arrest a working girl
than a woman belonging to the wealthier classes. On
this very occasion the police were heard to say, "We
want Kenny," meaning Miss Annie Kenny, the Lanca-
shire mill girl whose name was identified with the
W.S.P.U. from the outset. Miss Kenny had not taken
part in this particular demonstration at all, but she was
arrested all the same, although she was only present as
a spectator. The very different treatment accorded to
working-class women and those of another social status
made a very unfavourable impression on the public.
Lady Constance Lytton, when she was imprisoned in
her own name in 1909, was far more indulgently treated
than when she disguised herself as a working woman and
was arrested again under the name of Jane Warton.[1]

[1] See *Prison and Prisoners*, by Lady Constance Lytton.

I have in my possession a copy of a letter from the then Home Secretary, in which he says he will give special instructions to the police about my sister Mrs. Garrett Anderson (which could only be interpreted to mean that she was not to be arrested) on the occasion of one of the W.S.P.U. demonstrations, at which she had announced her intention of being present. But no preliminary warning had been given by Mrs. Cobden Sanderson and her friends, and, as I have said, no favour was shown to them by the police ; they even arrested one young girl who had taken no part in the demonstration.

Those who thought that these unusual proceedings would strike the Women's Suffrage Movement dead were soon proved to be wrong. The very reverse was the case. The secretaries and other active members of the older Suffrage Societies were worked off their feet ; every post brought applications for information and membership. Women's Suffrage was the topic of conversation in every household and at every social gathering ; the newspapers, too, were full of it. Money rolled in in an unexpected way ; where we were formerly receiving half-crowns and shillings, we were now getting £5 and £10 notes. One of my relatives (by marriage) said to me, " I was lukewarm, now I am boiling," and she was typical of thousands. It is not to be denied that some people sent cash as a practical expression of delight at anything that was damaging to the Government. For instance, a lady in Ireland from whom I had ordered my usual supply of bulbs for autumn planting, sent them, but without a bill, writing : " I do not send a bill ; give the money to those good women who are persecuting the Government." But there was also behind the movement the support of the innate political instinct of the British people. For instance, at one of our meetings, filled to suffocation so that we were obliged to get another hall for an overflow, the local M.P., one of our supporters, was present. He spoke in subdued and chastened tones of " recent events " and of " the very mistaken tactics which we so greatly deplore," and expressed the belief that the prisoners in Holloway, Mrs. Cobden Sanderson and her friends, " had deeply injured the Cause we all have at heart." Whereupon a working-man's voice was heard from the back of the hall, " They've rose the country, Sir," and this, with the aid afforded by the Government, was quite true.

Feeling as I did on the subject, I was often asked why I did not leave the Constitutional movement and become a militant. I asked myself this question very insistently, too. I was before all things desirous that we should keep our artillery for our opponents and not turn it on one another : on the other hand, I could not support a revolutionary movement, especially as it was ruled autocratically, at first, by a small group of four persons, and latterly by one person only ; the militant societies had, moreover, split into two, in 1907, chiefly on this question of the autocratic despotism with which the W.S.P.U. was ruled. In 1908 this despotism decreed that the policy of suffering violence, but using none, was to be abandoned. After that, I had no doubt whatever that what was right for me and the N.U.W.S.S. was to keep strictly to our principle of supporting our movement only by argument, based on common sense and experience and not by personal violence or law-breaking of any kind. It remained quite true that far more violence was suffered by the Suffragettes than they inflicted on their opponents. I will mention two instances : The turning of a hose upon a Suffrage prisoner in her cell on a mid-winter night in Strangeways Gaol, Manchester, because she had barricaded herself into her cell. This was not only disgraceful torture, it led to even more tragic consequences. The other was the throwing downstairs, by the stewards at a Liberal meeting at Bradford, of a man who had dared to support the militant women. His leg was broken, and he brought an action claiming damages at the Leeds Assizes in March 1911, and was awarded £100. I must mention here what I myself have seen, and a sickening and terrible sight it was : Suffragettes being carried by main force out of an Albert Hall meeting : a girl violently struggling, but powerless in the clutches of four men, two to her shoulders and two to her feet, and while in this defenceless position violently smitten on the face by enraged male members of the Liberal Party : both fists and umbrellas were used in this cowardly assault.

When Mrs. Cobden Sanderson and her companions were sentenced to two months' imprisonment in October 1906, I sought and obtained an interview with her in Holloway Gaol. I first saw the governor, a courteous old gentleman, who told me I could not see my friend in her cell, but could be shown another cell which exactly resembled it. I was put in charge of a wardress, who had orders to show me everything in the prison. I was first taken to the cell exactly resembling the one in which my friend was shut up—a long narrow slip of a room : the bed and bedding were rolled up in a tight bundle and placed perpendicularly against the wall, so that the bed could not be used as a couch : the window was small and very high up, just under the ceiling, so that little or nothing was visible from it : there was no chair, only a small narrow bench without back or sides. I asked the wardress if a chair was never provided. She replied with some asperity that the ratepayers (pronounced " rite-pires ") could not be expected to provide " luxuries " for the prisoners, adding, however, as an after-thought, that the prisoners were provided with luxuries ; I made no comment on this, but I did not forget it. I saw the workroom, the chapel, the infirmary, the exercise yard, and then was taken for my interview with Mrs. Cobden Sanderson. I had brought her a few flowers ; she was not allowed to accept them, but I observed with satisfaction that the mere handling of them for a moment appeared to give her pleasure. The wardress, of course, was present all through. My friend, whom I had always seen most daintily and charmingly dressed, was in the coarse and clumsy prison garb marked with the broad arrow. She had a dark-coloured coarse cloth hanging from her waist. " What is this ? " I asked, taking hold of it. She laughed, and said it was her handkerchief. No pockets were allowed, and this cloth, which was virtually a duster, was fastened to her side. She said it was lucky she had not a cold, as the allowance was only one a week. I believe it was one of the regulations that the prisoners were allowed neither pockets nor garters. She was a vegetarian, and her dinner in prison consisted of three potatoes. However, the doctor had recently ordered her two ounces of butter daily. " That makes an enormous difference," she said, cheerfully. She uttered no syllable of complaint or dissatisfaction. I thought of : "As shines the moon in cloudy skies, she in her poor attire was seen." One word would open her prison door. That word she refused to speak. There was a light in her eyes, a self-forgetting enthusiasm in her voice that cheered and refreshed me. She had done nothing morally wrong, and she was sustained by the belief that what she was enduring would hasten the day of women's freedom. When I left her, the wardress asked me if there was anything else I wished to see. " Yes," I replied, " I should like to see the luxuries you spoke of just now." The woman was for the moment taken aback, but could not deny her statement that the prisoners were provided with luxuries. She stammered that the luxury provided for the inhabitants of Holloway was cleanliness.

After what I had seen and heard I and a few friends determined to make what it is now the fashion to call " a gesture " of friendliness to the prisoners when they left Holloway, and I sent out on my personal responsibility the following letter :

November 1906.

(*Private.*)

It has been felt by many of the old workers for Women's Suffrage that the cause for which they have patiently laboured for so many years has received a great impetus from the courage and self-sacrifice of the group of women now undergoing a term of two months' imprisonment in Holloway Gaol in connection with the disturbance in the Lobby of the House of Commons on 23rd October.

I need hardly say that I am convinced that the work of quiet persuasion and argument form the solid foundation on which the success of the Women's Suffrage Movement will be reared ; and I, in common with the great majority of Suffrage workers, wish to continue the agitation on constitutional lines : yet we feel that the action of the prisoners has touched the imagination of the country in a manner which quieter methods did not succeed in doing. Many of us desire, therefore, to offer the prisoners some public mark of the value we attach to their self-sacrificing devotion, and with this end in view it is proposed to invite them to a banquet, the date of which will be fixed as soon as it is known when they will be released from prison.

It has been ascertained that they would accept such an invitation as soon as they are in a position to do so.

A fairly numerous General Committee will be formed to promote this project, and from their numbers a small Executive Committee will be selected and will be responsible for making all the necessary arrangements.

May I ask if you will give us the help and support of your name on the General Committee ? An early answer is requested.

Yours very faithfully,

(*Signed*)   MILLICENT GARRETT FAWCETT.

The banquet took place in December, and was a brilliant success, but, as was to be expected, my share in promoting it was severely criticized in many quarters, including my own Society. What had moved me as much as anything to make a public demonstration in support of the prisoners was the unscrupulous abuse and misrepresentation to which they had been subjected in the Press. I had known Mrs. Cobden Sanderson for many years, ever since she was a child, and when I read, in an account of the police-court proceedings, that she bit and scratched and screamed, I found the statement absolutely incredible. Miss Elizabeth Robins, the well-known authoress, who had been in the court, confirmed my incredulity by the positive statement that there was no sign of wild or hysterical excitement on the part of the prisoners, and added that what had been written about them was " extraordinarily and flagrantly untrue."

Chapter XIX

RAPID PROGRESS OF
THE SUFFRAGE MOVEMENT

MEANWHILE THE MOVEMENT for the enfranchisement of women made rapid progress in the country : the old societies had new life poured into them : many new societies were being formed. We, the old stagers, adopted new methods, one of the most successful of which was the organization of public processions in the streets : assembling at a given spot on the Embankment or in Trafalgar Square and marching, with banners flying and bands playing, to the Albert Hall, or some other time-honoured rendezvous. A day or two before our first procession I met a headmistress of one of our great girls' schools, a warm friend of our movement and a woman of sensitive refinement. " You will walk in our procession, Miss X," I remarked cheerfully. She replied, " I hate and loath the very thought of it, but of course I will be there," and I felt greatly encouraged. This first procession was on the 9th February 1907. The London weather did its worst against us ; mud, mud, mud, as its predominant feature, and it was known among us afterwards as the " mud march." Between 3,000 and 4,000 law-abiding women tramped through the streets to testify their demand for their share in the government of their country. But our Bill was talked out in the House of Commons, the Speaker refusing the closure. The next year, 1908, we again had a street procession, and this time the sun shone upon us and I believe we made a really favourable impression on the crowd of onlookers. It was reckoned that the procession was 15,000 strong. We were indebted to our friend Mrs. (now Lady) Herringham for a generous gift of most beautiful Indian silks to make our banners, and to Miss Mary Lowndes, more than to any other person, for their design, correct heraldry, and arrangement. I believe few more beautiful street scenes can have been witnessed in London than this procession afforded. The Albert Hall, decorated with our banners under Miss Lowndes' guidance, became a fairy palace of beauty. My old friend Lady Dorothy Nevill wrote to congratulate me on this procession. She said, " I saw it in Piccadilly from a window there : it was all too wonderful, and you have my best wishes." She added that some time back " by misadventure " she had allowed her name to be added to a list of Anti-Suffragists, " a thing I now deplore, and I have written to say my name must be withdrawn." Our objective at this procession was the Albert Hall. I was in the chair, and by a pretty thought, unrevealed to me beforehand, the processionists came provided with bunches of summer flowers, which they deposited in front of me on the platform until I was almost buried in them, and I felt like Freia behind the mass of the Nibelungen treasure. Mr. W. D. Howells, the well-known American author, was one of the spectators of this procession. He wrote enthusiastically about it to the American papers, and made use of the expression, " There are many arguments against it (the women's vote) but no reasons." But it must not be supposed that the comments made upon us were all complimentary. One stern-looking and very long-legged man walked rapidly down our lines facing us and saying from time to time, " Yes, yes, all one type, all alike, all old maids." One small boy was also convinced that none of us had ever found a man bold enough to wed us, and addressing himself especially to Lady Strachey, who was walking, tall and stately, at the head of our procession, said, " Wouldn't yer like to get a 'usband ? " Looking down on him, Lady Strachey replied, " Not wishing to commit bigamy, I should not."

This year, 1908, we got a second reading for our Bill in the House of Commons, as we did in 1909, 1910, and 1911. But the hostility of the Liberal Government barred all further progress. In 1908 the N.U.W.S.S. made a definite break with the W.S.P.U. on account of the latter having finally abandoned the policy which they had at first adopted of suffering violence but using none. Stone-throwing, window-breaking, and other forms of violence were organized by the W.S.P.U., and we felt we had no choice but to publish protests against everything of this kind. We also had to take means to exclude the Militant Suffragists from membership of our societies. Those who wish to know more in detail about the situation at this time between ourselves and the militants are referred to Chapter VI of a little book I wrote in 1911, called *Women's Suffrage : A Short History of a Great Movement* (T. C. and E. C. Jack, London and Edinburgh). To put the whole matter in a sentence, we were convinced that our job was to win the hearts and minds of our countrymen to the justice of our cause, and that this could never be done by force and violence :

> Men must reap the things they sow,
> Force from force must ever flow.

We had seen force ever leading to more and more violent force in Ireland, in Russia, and other places, and felt certain that our movement would be no exception to this rule. This conviction led our society to ever greater activity on the lines of constitutional action.

In 1910 a committee known as the Conciliation Committee was formed, mainly through the efforts of its president, Lord Lytton, and its hon. secretary, Mr. H. N. Brailsford, to draft a Women's Suffrage Bill which would conciliate the greatest possible number of Suffragists in and out of Parliament. One important achievement of this committee was to induce the militant societies to desist from violence, and threats of violence, so as to give the Bill every possible chance of passing through all its stages in the House of Commons. I do not dwell upon the activities of the Conciliation Committee, as they have been described by me elsewhere (see *The Women's Victory*, Sidgwick and Jackson), but its object was to bring together all the supporters of women's enfranchisement in the Houses of Parliament and by frank and full discussion to arrive at the greatest common measure of agreement between them. It is well known that the main object of the Conciliation Committee was never attained. Still, looking back on the whole situation as it developed, especially after the outbreak of the Great War, I believe that it had its share in preparing the country for the conciliation of parties which led to the final triumph. It was also through the Conciliation Committee that our question got its first serious hearing in the House of Lords, where a Women's Suffrage Bill was introduced by Lord Selborne in May 1914, and when Lord Lytton made a most memorable and moving speech on its behalf.

I am tempted here to insert "what I remember" of an interview I had with Mr. Lloyd George in his official residence in Downing Street. I cannot recall the exact date, but it was in 1910, some month or so after the first of the two General Elections of that year.

My line was to press on him the absolute necessity of Government support for a reasonable measure of Women's Franchise. His line was that this was rendered impossible in consequence of " militancy." He called upon me as President of the N.U.W.S.S. to put a stop to it. I replied that this again was an impossibility, and I asked him how he imagined we could stop militancy when he and the whole Government of which he was a member had had no success in their efforts in the same direction. " You," I said, " have the whole resources of the Government behind you : a police force of many thousands at your beck and call : a bottomless purse to draw upon : but you have not succeeded in stopping it, and why should you expect us to succeed when you, with these enormous advantages, have failed ? There is only one way of stopping militancy, and that is to grant the justice of the claim of women to representation and to give facilities for a Suffrage Bill." He evinced some impatience at this reply, but evaded the issue and repeated that militancy was alienating support from our Cause in every direction. " There is my wife, for instance, originally a warm supporter of women's franchise, now quite estranged from it. What's to be done ? The Government can do nothing while this folly lasts."

I replied : " Mr. Lloyd George, a few weeks ago I was in Carnarvon [his own constituency], where we had a very successful Suffrage meeting. The next day my friends took me to see the sights of the town. On our way towards the Castle we passed down a good street where I saw a very handsome house which had every pane of every window smashed to atoms. I naturally asked an explanation, and was then told that the house was the Conservative Club and that the damage had been done by your friends and supporters just after the recent election, and that they had done this, not because they were angry, but because they were pleased by your triumphant return. I inquired what punishment the rioters had received : had they been imprisoned or fined ? The answer was that no punishment had been inflicted.

The ringleaders, I was told, had been duly charged and brought before the magistrate, but that he had declined to consider the case seriously, and had said ' that allowance must be made for political excitement.' Why is allowance made for political excitement in the case of men who can and do express their feelings at the ballot-box, but no allowance is made in the case of women when they are excited by political injustice and are driven to express their indignation by acts of violence ? " Of course there was no answer to this inquiry, but Mr. Lloyd George deftly turned the subject and said he wished to introduce me to his wife.

I think I ought to make some reference to the encouragement given to our work by the Anti-Suffrage organization. At first they had two societies, one for men and one for women. It occurred to them that amalgamation of these was desirable, and a meeting was announced in London at which this amalgamation was to be carried out. Mrs. Humphry Ward excused herself from attendance on account of her preoccupation in helping her son, who was fighting a contested election. It was characteristic even of the ablest of the Anti-Suffragists to see no inconsistency in proclaiming that there would be " immeasurable injury done by bringing women into political life " and freely engaging in it herself. Our younger members took a great delight in attending Anti-Suffrage meetings : one of them wrote to me in July 1910 :

" I don't know when I have enjoyed anything so much as the Antis' meeting in Trafalgar Square yesterday. There was a very slim crowd of Antis, a certain number of onlookers, and quite as many Suffragists as Antis. We were all in the highest spirits and the Antis very glum. We disposed of hundreds of our ' Pass the Bill ' badges and had to send back to the office for more. I tried to get some of their Anti-Suff. literature, but they wouldn't give me any. At last, to my delight, a woman wearing an Anti badge presented me with a pamphlet . . . but it turned out to be about the English being the lost tribes of Israel ! " . . . Then comes a passage describing the decorations : " flimsy little *cotton* flags *lying down* on each of the three sides of plinth. It is of a piece with their general futility to have chosen black and pink for their colours which can't be got in bunting."

A working-man's comment on the Anti-Suffrage colours was told me by another of my young friends : " Pink for gentility," with intense scorn conveyed by the last word, " and black for the funeral, for y've got a dying cause."

It was a year or two before this that invitations of an unusual nature reached me to speak on Votes for Women. One was from the President of the Oxford Union Debating Society, Mr. M. H. Richmond, to put the case for the political enfranchisement of women before the Society. This was in 1908, and in 1909 I was asked to take part in a public debate at the Passmore Edwards Settlement, with Mrs. Humphry Ward as my antagonist. There was a refreshing novelty about these invitations, and I accepted them unhesitatingly. I am not sure that I appreciated at the time the degree to which the invitation to speak at the Oxford Union was an innovation ; but an article by Mr. G. E. C. Bodley on the Centenary of the Union, published in December 1923, describes the Jubilee of the Union in 1873, and refers to the presence of the President's father, adding, " It was the only time I ever heard a non-resident or a stranger speak at the Union." When to the disqualifications of being neither a resident, nor a graduate, nor an under-graduate, I added the further damning fact of being of the wrong sex, I can appreciate now, better than I did at the time, the generosity which prevailed among the young men who gave me so warm a welcome to the Society. At Oxford I was the guest of Mr. and Mrs. Sidney Ball, of St. John's House. Needless to say that with such hosts I had a delightful time, and the debate went off with perfect order and good temper. I heard no new arguments either for or against Suffrage, but it was very cheering to see the hall and galleries packed and to witness the great interest our question was arousing in the University. Among my supporters were the two sons of Lord Selborne, who formerly, as Lord Wolmer, had been our very able and courteous leader in the House of Commons. The Chairman of the meeting was, of course, the President of the Union, Mr. M. H. Richmond, of New College. The resolution moved by Mr. R. A. Knox, of Balliol, was : " That in the opinion of this House the time has come when the Government should be urged to remove the electoral disabilities of women." When the voting came the Ayes were 329 and the Noes 360, therefore we were defeated in a House of nearly 700 members by 31 : and almost everyone who spoke to me on the subject assured me that this majority, such as it was, did not represent undergraduate feeling, but that a considerable number of the older members of the University who are entitled to be present, although they very seldom avail themselves of the privilege, had turned the scale by their votes. If undergraduates only had voted, I was assured there would have been a considerable majority for Women's Suffrage. I was glad to learn that youth had been on our side. But, in fact, the result appeared to please everyone, and when the figures were read out there was much cheering and counter-cheering : everyone was pleased : we, by the narrow margin against us and its composition, while our opponents enjoyed the solid satisfaction that always attends the winning of a division. The next morning we were photographed together, the committee of the Union, Mr. Sidney Ball, and myself, in the court of St. John's College, and it is a satisfaction to me even now to see, sitting in the lowest row in the photograph, the charming young figure of Mr. Robert Palmer, Lord Selborne's second son.   Before his short life was ended, he did quite splendid work for our cause in the two fields of Suffrage for Women and the establishment of an equal moral standard, or some approach to it, for men and women.   We lost a great political leader when he was killed quite early in the war, for he had courage, industry, enthusiasm, and the guiding principle of strong religious faith.   His life, written by Lady Laura Ridding, is a record of what he actually accomplished ; and also shows what his country and the world, too, was losing month by month and year by year by the cutting short of these beautiful young lives.

My debate with Mrs. Humphry Ward at the Passmore Edwards Settlement in February in 1909 had no such tragic sequel.   I do not know if I should have made any mention of it here if it had not been that in her life of her Mother, Mrs. G. M. Trevelyan, quite unintentionally of course, rather conveyed the impression that it was a packed meeting, and that the result of the vote was therefore a foregone conclusion.   The facts were these :   the hall, which holds about 500 people, was crowded ; the tickets were sold at a good price, and the total proceeds of the sale were by mutual agreement given to the New (now the Elizabeth Garrett Anderson) Hospital for Women.   Not one ticket was given away on our side.   Mrs. Humphry Ward desired from the outset to reserve 150 tickets—that is, nearly a third of the whole—for herself and her friends : the remainder were sold by Miss McKee, the President, and Mrs. Bertram, the secretary of the St. Pancras branch of the N.U.W.S.S., to every applicant, without inquiry as to the views of those who asked for them, but strictly in the order in which the application had been received.   Mrs. Ward

said in a note she wrote on the subject immediately
after the meeting, that she had tried to reserve her 150
tickets for Anti-Suffragists ; but nothing of a corre-
sponding nature was done by the Suffragists, and we
were surprised as well as pleased by the large majority
by which we won. The figures were 235 to 74, and I
gathered that Mrs. Ward was also surprised and not
only surprised, but displeased, for she said to me with
vehemence in the little room at the back of the platform
to which we were both shepherded when the meeting
was over, " I shall *never* do this sort of thing again,
never, and I shall write to the papers to say so." My
impression was that a considerable number of the Anti-
Suffragists present had never before heard the Suffrage
case fairly presented, and that on hearing it they either
changed their vote or did not vote at all. We have
reason to know that votes were changed as a result of
the speeches and the discussion that followed. Mrs.
Ward, in the note already quoted, said : " We tried to
reserve ours for Anti-Suffragists, but as a matter of fact
a good many were distributed without questions asked,
and of my own eight, three were neutral and two voted
against me." Miss McKee and Mrs. Bertram sent a
letter to the Press a day or two after the meeting setting
out these facts, and no one disputed the accuracy of
their statement. We had Sir Edward Busk, LL.B.,
an able and experienced chairman, to preside over the
meeting. Mrs. Humphry Ward, at her own request,
opened the debate with a written paper and I replied :
to each of us was then allotted the same number of minutes
for further exposition of our case : then a general discussion followed, in which members of the audience
joined. Great was our pleasure when Sir Johnston
Forbes-Robertson spoke in our support. I shall not
easily forget the delight to my ears of his silvery voice.
I think I should have enjoyed it even if he had spoken

against us—but not so much. Then Mrs. Ward and I each had four or five minutes to reply, and the vote was taken with the result already mentioned. I may add that the sum for which the tickets had been sold was sufficient to qualify both Mrs. Humphry Ward and Miss McKee to become life governors of the Hospital. I was a life governor already, so I gladly made way for the other two ladies.

Chapter XX

THE DEFEAT OF THE CONCILIATION BILL: ITS CAUSES AND CONSEQUENCES

As a preliminary to this chapter of " What I Remember " I must remind my readers that our greatest enemy in the Liberal Party was the Prime Minister, Mr. Asquith. We were constantly pushing as hard as we could, and in cordial co-operation with the forward Suffrage group in the Women's Liberal Federation and the Conservative and Unionist W.S. Association over which the Countess of Selborne presided, to get a Suffrage Bill carried in Parliament and placed upon the Statute Book, before Mr. Asquith got his chance of passing a Manhood Suffrage Bill. We thought, and he, no doubt, agreed, that Manhood Suffrage, if carried, would place a tremendous obstacle in the way of our success, because neither the House nor the country was prepared at one blow for the creation of an electorate of which more than half would be women. A truce from militancy had been procured, mainly through Mr. Brailsford's influence, for nearly two years, i.e. from January 1910 to November 1911. In that interval the second reading of the Conciliation Bill was carried twice, first by a majority of 110, and later by a majority of 167. There would have been ample Parliamentary time to proceed with it, but of course nothing was further from the Prime Minister's intention than to allow this. On the contrary, the Bill was " torpedoed," to use

Mr. Lloyd George's expression, by Mr. Asquith promising, on 7th November 1911, a large measure of electoral reform basing the franchise on citizenship to be extended to "all persons of full age and competent understanding," but doing nothing for women. When asked by Mr. Henderson about this, the Prime Minister replied curtly that his views on this subject were well known, and had suffered no modification or change in recent years. The whole Suffrage world strongly resented the tactics which had been employed against them. If Mr. Asquith desired to revive a violent outbreak of militancy he could not have acted differently or done more to promote his end. We were furiously angry, but not so blinded by our anger as to be incapable of playing our hand in the next stage of the game. There was a joint deputation of all the Suffrage Societies to Mr. Asquith on 18th November 1911, and we extracted the following pledges from him :

1. That the Government would use its utmost endeavours to get the Reform Bill carried through in all its stages during the session of 1912.

2. That it should be so drafted as to admit of Women's Suffrage amendments.

3. That the Government would not officially oppose such amendments.

4. That such amendments, if carried in the Commons, would be accepted by the Government as an integral part of the Bill, and defended in all its subsequent stages in both Houses of Parliament.

That is how the stage was set, so far as our question was concerned, at the opening of the session of 1912. The whole strength and energy of the Anti-Suffrage section in the House, especially the Anti-Suffrage Liberals, was concentrated on the defeat of the Conciliation Bill. And they were successful in March 1912.

Our disappointment was intense. We had thought that now, at least, after nearly forty years of work, we had a definite prospect of success. So did Sir Edward Grey, who had used the expression : that we now had " a real opportunity " and " not a bogus offer." We did not foresee that the very fact that we had wrested these promises from Mr. Asquith had made his faithful henchmen more than ever determined that they should not be fulfilled. One of these wrote a letter to the Press calling upon the followers of Mr. Asquith in the House not to subject their leader to the " humiliation " of having to fulfil his promises. The way to rescue him, it was pointed out, was to defeat the Conciliation Bill on second reading. But there were other and even less creditable ways of working against us ; prominent members of the Liberal Party by stealthy manœuvring sought to detach whole blocks of our supporters from fulfilling their pledges to us. They were remarkably successful, especially with the Irish Nationalists. The way the trick was done was described by Mr. T. P. O'Connor, M.P., in an article in the *Chicago Tribune*. A Liberal master of intrigue, sauntering through the tea-room, would see a group of Irish Nationalists and stop and enter into conversation with them, and would presently observe what a pity it was that the work for the Irish Home Rule Bill would be thrown away after all, as, of course, if the Conciliation Bill were carried on the second reading, and the Prime Minister consequently compelled to fulfil his promises about it, the Government would break up and goodness knew what reactionary Government would come into power, and where would Home Rule be then ? As a result of these intrigues, thirty Irish Nationalists who had supported our Bill were entirely detached from it, and most of them voted against it ; three only stood firm : Mr. W. O'Brien, Mr. T. Healy, and Mr. Gilhooley.

If this was the sort of thing Liberalism stood for in 1912, it was little wonder that it showed other symptoms of decay at a later date. But however brought about, the defeat of the Bill with the destruction of the hopes we had formed in respect to it, was a great blow to us. A member of his family told me it had literally killed Walter MacLaren. He was ill at the time, and the bitter disappointment turned the scale against him and he died. We never had a more devoted and loyal friend. Mr. Asquith was naturally delighted at our defeat, and on 12th July 1912, in his elation at our discomfiture, he said, in the second reading debate on his own Reform Bill, " This Bill does not propose to confer the franchise on women : whatever extension of the franchise it makes is to male persons only " ; and referring to the defeat of the Conciliation Bill in the previous month he added, " I dismiss as altogether improbable the hypothesis that the House of Commons is likely to stultify itself by reversing in the same session the considered judgment at which it has arrived." Considering the means which had been taken to defeat the Conciliation Bill, and that this defeat was only accomplished by 14 votes, this almost surpassed in arrogance and effrontery what one had become accustomed to expect from the Liberal Prime Minister. One result of Mr. Asquith's words even so experienced a Parliamentarian as he did not foresee. The interminable session of 1912 spread itself out into 1913, and it was not until January of that year that the Committee stage of the Government Reform Bill was reached. It then appeared that Mr. Asquith's words of the preceding July had really dug the grave of his own Bill. In answer to a question raised by Mr. Bonar Law, the Speaker raised the objection that the Bill then before the House was not the same Bill which had been read a second time in July. This judgment he based on the Government's own amendments to the Bill, regarding the occupation franchise ; but he added that there were " other amendments regarding female suffrage which, of course, would make a large difference to the Bill if they were inserted." The Speaker's ruling killed the Government Bill ; to go on with it was impossible, to withdraw it and re-introduce it in an altered form was at that period of the session also impossible. It became known as the Government fiasco of 1913. Deep as our anger was against the Prime Minister, his tricks and his manners, it did not prevent us from having our little jokes on the subject. Our beloved Lady Strachey sent me on the appropriate date the following quotation from *Paradise Lost*, as a suggested Valentine for Mr. Asquith :

> And by proof we feel
> Our powers sufficient to disturb his Heaven,
> And with perpetual inroads to alarm,
> Though inaccessible, his fatal throne,
> Which if not victory is yet revenge.

This was too good to part with, and I have kept it among my papers, where I see it from time to time, and use it as a refreshment.

After our disappointment over the Government Bill, the militants broke out into renewed fury, smashing shop and office windows all down the best-known streets of London, as well as attacking Government offices and the private houses of obnoxious individuals. They overwhelmed Mr. Brailsford with reproaches for having induced them to suspend their methods of violence for nearly two years in order to give the Conciliation Bill a chance.

I remember what I felt when I heard the bad news of the defeat of the Bill. I was one of a crowd of some hundreds of women walking up and pacing down Palace Yard and Parliament Square on that March evening. I felt that what I had been working for for forty years had been destroyed at a blow ; but I also felt what beavers feel when their dam has been destroyed, namely, that they must begin all over again, and build it up once more from the beginning. While I was in that frame of mind I met Mr. Stead. It was the last time I ever saw him, for the *Titanic* disaster followed in two or three weeks. He spoke some cheering words to me, but I was at a point when cheering words were meaningless, and I remained in a state of great depression from which I had much difficulty in rousing myself.

One of the results of the defeat of the Bill and the machinations that had brought it about was that the N.U.W.S.S. gave a new definition to its election policy. Hitherto our policy at by-elections had been to work, irrespective of party, for the return of the best friend of Women's Suffrage, and this continued to be our policy, but we decided, after finding that forty-two " best friends " had voted against us, not only to take account of the various personal declarations of the candidates, but also of the attitude of the party to which they severally owed allegiance. This meant that in all contests where a Labour man was standing we should prefer him, if his personal position was sound, to members of the other parties which were either neutral or hostile to our cause. This, of course, was because Labour was the only party definitely supporting Women's Suffrage. Our attitude was attacked as a departure from our non-party attitude. I strongly dissented from this view. In finding out which of a group of candidates was our best friend, it was plain common sense to take account of the position of their several parties, as well as their personal declarations. A Suffragist who belonged to a Suffrage party was a better friend than a Suffragist who belonged to a party which was Anti-Suffrage or neutral. There were some exceptions to this rule : men such as Lord Robert Cecil among the Conservatives, and Mr.

Walter MacLaren and Mr. W. H. Dickinson among the Liberals, on whose support we could absolutely depend, no matter what opposition was offered by their parties. Therefore we excepted " tried friends " from the operation of our revised definition. But we defined afresh the general objects of the N.U.W.S.S. in by-elections :

1. To shorten the term of office of the Cabinet as at present constituted, especially by opposing Anti-Suffrage Ministers, and

2. To strengthen any party in the House which adopted Women's Suffrage as part of its official programme.

At by-elections we supported no Government candidate, and no candidate who did not answer all the N.U.W.S.S. questions in the affirmative. I well remember the glee with which we pursued some of the wobblers who had tried to make the best of both worlds by offering words to us during elections, but votes on all critical occasions on the altar of their party. This new development of our work was called the Election Fighting Policy, and to support it we raised a special fund, called the Election Fighting Fund. At the Council meeting, when it was proposed and adopted, £2,000 was subscribed in the room, and this sum was spent and renewed many times before the Great War came and stopped all electoral activities.

As soon as it was initiated, we had satisfactory interviews with leading members of the Labour Party on the subject. We explained our position, that we had not abandoned our non-party attitude; if, for instance, another party made Women's Suffrage part of its programme, we should have to revise our position ; the N.U.W.S.S. and the Labour representatives were in complete agreement about maintaining, on both sides, absolute independence. When we went into constituencies to support a Labour man, we ran our own organization, had our own meetings and speakers, paid our own expenses. We selected from among our best speakers those who were in sympathy with the views of Labour. This plan had been brought to our notice, and strongly recommended to us, by Mr. H. N. Brailsford. He said in effect, " The Liberal leaders treat you with contempt now ; but show them that you have power to move members from one side of the House to the other, and they will immediately become more respectful." This prophecy was very soon fulfilled. The E.F.F. had not been in existence a month before it was put to work ; and in Holmfirth, Hanley, Crewe, and Midlothian the Election Fighting Fund and its band of organizers and speakers were in active operation in support of Labour candidates in 1912. The next year, 1913, we fought elections in Houghton-le-Spring, Keighley, and Lanark ; and in 1914 in North-West Durham, Leith Burghs, and North-East Derbyshire. There were therefore ten elections during the two years in which the E.F.F. policy was worked by us, and in these we gave effective help in the transference of six of them from the Liberal to the Conservative side of the House. This, of course, made a difference of twelve in a division, and we rejoiced accordingly. One of my friends, a Conservative, who had taken part in the Council meeting at which the E.F.F. policy was adopted, came to me when it was over, and almost with tears said she felt she must leave us. I endeavoured to dissuade her but, as I then thought, without effect. However, some eighteen months later, happening to meet her in London, I said, " You ought never to have left us," and she rejoined, " Well, I never did ! "

Besides this effective election work we also, in 1913, made by far our most successful effort in the way of publicity and advertisement by what we called the "Pilgrimage." This originated in the active mind of our colleague, Mrs. Harley, president of our Shrewsbury society. Our nineteen Federations were in full swing and full working order, raising for our cause quite £45,000 a year ; we were provided with a splendid band of organizers, young women mostly of University training and first-class abilities. They did admirable propaganda work up and down the country and, moreover, kept Headquarters well informed upon all local developments and incidents bearing upon our movement. With their help we undertook the Pilgrimage, which was a march of non-militant Suffragists from every part of England and Wales, converging on London on a given day. Eight routes were selected—the Great North Road, the Fen Country, the East Coast Road, Watling Street, the West Country Road, the Portsmouth Road, the Brighton Road, and the Kentish Pilgrim's Way. The Pilgrims journeyed on foot with occasional lifts, friends lending motors for luggage and the less robust of the Pilgrims. The whole thing caught on to a tremendous extent ; villagers ran out to meet us, begging us to stop and give them a meeting ; all kinds of hospitality were offered and gratefully accepted. When once .people understood that we had no desire to hurt anybody nor to damage anything, they gave us a most cordial reception. The final demonstration was held in Hyde Park on 26th July. There were nineteen platforms, representing our nineteen Federations ; as I approached my own there was a large crowd in front of it, and I rather wondered how I should get through and mount my wagon, when a man, whom I had not noticed before, seemed to spring up out of the earth, and, walking by my side, made way for me. I did not speak to him, but I just thought, " I wonder who you are." He, answering my thought, said, " Plain clothes officer, m'm." It was all like a wonderful dream, and so was our service the next day in St. Paul's with Canon Simpson preaching a sermon for us, and as far as my eye could reach the friendly faces of thousands of dear friends and fellow-workers greeted me from every part of the great cathedral. What luck for us that it was the 27th day of the month, and we had the wonderful and appropriate Psalm, " When the Lord turned again the captivity of Sion, then were we like unto them that dream."

We had a deputation to Mr. Asquith within the next few days ; he amused us by his politeness, and was quite complimentary about the Pilgrimage. It was then that I could not resist saying to him that I had never seen a man so much improved. Mr. Brailsford's recipe for good manners had been in active operation for nearly two years.

Chapter XXI

THE RISE OF THE LABOUR PARTY AND OTHER
ENCOURAGING CIRCUMSTANCES

DURING ALL THE DIFFICULT but encouraging times through which we were passing in the years immediately preceding the Great War we were battling with Mr. Asquith in defence of the elementary principles of his own party, while he, with great ingenuity and resource, was battling against them. During these anxious times, when the final issue seemed to hang in the balance, we received very great help and encouragement from the leaders of the Labour Party. I would mention particularly in this connection the names of Mr. Philip Snowden, Mr. Ramsay MacDonald, Mr. Keir Hardie, Mr. W. C. Anderson, and Mr. Arthur Henderson. First came a resolution adopted at the Labour Conference in London in 1912, to the effect that any Government Reform Bill for the further representation of men would be " inacceptable " to the Labour Party if it did not also include women : when we asked exactly what " inacceptable " meant, we learnt, with joy, that it was equivalent to " would not be accepted." This attitude was emphasized a little later. At a moment of deep discouragement on our part, after the fiasco of the Government Reform Bill of January 1913, and when Mr. Asquith and his satellites were offering us the absolutely worthless alternative of a day for a discussion of a Private Member's Bill, there was an important and representative session of the Labour

Party Conference. The resolution officially brought forward presented a not unusual blend of ambiguous and conflicting views, when Mr. Snowden rose to move an amendment which had been placed on the paper by the Fabian Society and the Women's Labour League. There was nothing ambiguous about this ; it ran thus : *" It further calls upon the Party in Parliament to oppose any Franchise Bill in which women are not included."* Those present describe the thrill that went through the audience as Mr. Snowden's speech proceeded. A card vote was demanded and intense excitement prevailed as the tellers went round. The result was : " For the amendment 870, against 437." That went a long way to console us for what we had suffered from Mr. Asquith and his Anti-Suffrage colleagues. The effect of the vote was to kill any Manhood Suffrage Bill which might have been intended by our opponents ; and every member of Mr. Asquith's Government realized that it had placed the idea of re-introducing a purely male franchise measure in the region of the impossible. The resolution of the Conference was a definite instruction which every member of the Party was bound to observe. This was followed in the ensuing September at the Trade Union Congress by a resolution censuring the Government for not fulfilling their promises to us, and demanding a Government Reform Bill which should include women. In the opinion of many competent observers the question of Women's Franchise now absolutely dominated home politics. The Chairman of the Labour Party, Mr. Ramsay MacDonald (now Prime Minister), spoke out very plainly : " We shall take care," he said, " that a Manhood Suffrage Bill is not used to destroy the success of the women's agitation, because we have to admit *that it has been the women's agitation that has brought the franchise both for men and women to the front at the present time."*

Mr. Keir Hardie attended the Congress of the International Women's Suffrage Alliance at Budapest in 1913, and did much to remove the apathy and ignorance of the Labour men there in regard to the significance of the women's agitation. All through this time, too, we were getting invaluable support from a section of the Home Press, chief among which I shall always remember the *Manchester Guardian*, which struck blow after blow, telling and well directed, in our support. The drama also was a great ally. Sir James Barrie's *What Every Woman Knows* and *The Admirable Crichton*, Mr. Shaw's *Androcles and the Lion*, besides many passages in other plays, were immeasurably helpful to us. At this time, looking forward, or trying to do so, into the future, I could see plainly that we were on the high road to success in the House of Commons ; but I was wholly baffled when I tried to imagine what power on earth, short of the Parliament Act, could get a Women's Franchise measure through the Lords. When Lord Selborne introduced an extremely mild Women's Suffrage Bill in the Lords in May 1914, we thought we had done well when it was only defeated by 104 to 60. And we had other consolations : Lord Lytton's magnificent speech, the support of the Archbishop of Canterbury and of all the Bishops present and voting, also scraps of overheard conversation from members of the House. One, which I heard myself during the Anti-Suffrage speech of Lord Charnwood, was from a middle-aged peer who looked the picture of an old-fashioned English country gentleman : he got up from his seat and flung out of the House, exclaiming as he passed me, " If I listened for another five minutes to this fellow I should vote for the Bill." Another I did not hear but only heard of. It was said to have been uttered by Lord Curzon : the story as told to me was that as Lord Lytton sat down Lord Curzon exclaimed, " What a tragedy that such talent should be wasted on women."

It was earlier than this—in November 1912—that,

feeling, I suppose, that Anti-Suffragism on its merits was not making much way in the House of Commons, other methods were tried. On the 21st November the Marquis of Tullibardine (now Duke of Atholl) asked the Home Secretary if his attention had been called to an " obscene pamphlet " sold by the National Union of Women's Suffrage Societies, and whether he would take any steps to prohibit its further sale or prosecute the N.U.W.S.S. Mr. McKenna replied that he had not been acquainted with the publication in question until his attention had been called to it by Lord Tullibardine, and that he would consider it. His answer indicated that the pamphlet was then in his possession. The little book in question, called *Under the Surface*,[1] is very short. Its aim was much the same as Flexner's well-known book, published by the Rockefeller Foundation, called the *History of Prostitution in Europe*. Its purpose was obvious to the meanest understanding, namely, to warn its readers against actions which are almost certain to involve suffering and degradation—national and personal. Its author was Dr. Louise Martindale, then of Brighton, a lady of the highest character and excellent professional standing, and greatly respected wherever she was known. Lord Tullibardine and Mr. McKenna between them kept up the question-and-answer game in the House of Commons on the lines above indicated for nearly a fortnight. Of course the lowest papers, which might be described, if I may paraphrase the words of St. Luke, " as lewd rags of the baser sort," made the utmost of the implied accusation against the N.U.W.S.S. I wrote to the Home Secretary on the subject and asked him if our Society

[1] Mr. R. F. Cholmley, Head Master of Dame Alice Owen's School, Islington, and afterwards President of the Head Masters' Association, wrote an excellent letter to the Press to the effect that his experience as a schoolmaster made him welcome the book as an invaluable assistance in the discharge of a most difficult part of a head master's duty to his boys.

and the writer of the pamphlet were to be for an indefinite period under the imputation of the intolerable insult implied in Lord Tullibardine's questions. I do not remember receiving an answer. Mr. McKenna was absent from the House when the reply to the offensive question was at length given : the Under-Secretary, Mr. Ellis Griffith, appeared, and said, " The Secretary of State is advised that the institution of proceedings would not be warranted in the case of this book." Pressed further by the Marquis, Mr. Griffith reiterated, " I am advised that a prosecution on these lines would not be successful." Mr. Snowden then intervened, asking with indignation if the Home Office accepted the insinuations implied in the questions. Lord Robert Cecil also spoke in the same sense and with good effect, but Mr. Griffith could not be driven from the perfectly safe position from which he had sheltered himself and his chief : he only reiterated, " We are advised that a prosecution, if instituted, would not be successful." Of course it would not. But I have always considered that the whole thing was a dastardly trick intended to discredit the women who were working for the political liberty of their own sex. This sort of thing had been tried a year or two earlier, in 1909, but in a more amateurish, hole-in-the-corner way. The procedure then was to whisper scandals against Suffragists in back drawing-rooms in Kensington to timid maiden ladies, who were told that the villainies perpetrated by the Suffragists were of so black a dye that details could not possibly be disclosed except to married women. It was a case of " I wants ter make y'r flesh creep," and it certainly in some instances had this desired effect. I was furious about it, especially as the culprits, when run to earth, tried to placate me by saying that those whom they were blackening were not members of " my " Society but of " Mrs. Pankhurst's." I did not care which

Society was being attacked in an absolutely unjustifiable way. I succeeded in stopping it, partly by appealing straight to Mrs. Humphry Ward and partly by letting the guilty scandal-mongers know that it was not improbable that legal proceedings would be instituted against them.

Another of the difficulties connected with this period lay in the fact that the W.S.P.U., not content with the autocratic control of their own followers, also tried to control ours. They deliberately endeavoured to limit our choice of speakers to such as they approved. For some reason which was never disclosed they had a vendetta against Mr. Henderson (the present Home Secretary). At a big Albert Hall meeting held by us in February 1914 he was one of our speakers ; as soon as he rose an organized uproar was started with the object of drowning his voice, under the personal direction of a well-known leader of the Suffragettes. But they had reckoned without their host. Mr. Henderson held his own splendidly. He has at command a gigantic voice, and as the shrill cries of the Suffragettes rose he first changed his pitch, drew out another stop, as it were, from the big organ of his vocal chords, flung out his voice at its loudest and went on undisturbed, unhurried, without ever losing the thread of his argument or taking the slightest notice of the riot. He never lost his temper nor his nerve, and the consequence was that instead of overwhelming him in confusion, exactly the contrary effect was produced : everyone in the hall became aware that they were witnessing the pluckiest performance that they had ever seen at a public meeting, and as he sat down the audience rose at him, clapping and singing " For he's a Jolly Good Fellow."

After this, with the exception of one belated effort made after the Suffrage campaign had ended in victory, we had no more trouble with attempted Suffragette interference in our choice of speakers. But this belongs to the events of 1918.

Chapter XXII

THE GREAT WAR AND WOMEN'S WAR WORK

TUESDAY, THE 4TH AUGUST 1914, will never be forgotten by any of us. The previous day had been Bank Holiday, but there was no holiday feeling in the air. All day long masses of men and women of all classes tramped solemnly, silently, and sorrowfully along Whitehall and Parliament Street, waiting and hoping for news that would relieve their anxiety and suspense. Our committee was sitting all that day, and we were trying to devise plans for keeping our organization in being—notwithstanding what we felt in the event of war to be absolutely necessary—the entire suspension of our political work. The actual declaration of war took place at 11 p.m. on 4th August, and on Thursday, 6th August, we had pretty well agreed on a course of action. We could not summon our six hundred societies to a Council, the railways were wanted for other work than ours, but we consulted our societies by post and laid before them our views, on which we asked their comment and hoped for their co-operation. The absence from home of secretaries and presidents of our societies, owing to the holiday season, prevented many of them from replying to our inquiries. But of those we did hear from, all but two agreed to our proposals. So far as I can remember, the Executive Committee was unanimous in declaring that the ordinary political work of the Society must necessarily be suspended during the war ; but we felt that we should use our organization and our money-raising powers for the relief of the distress caused by the dislocation of business brought about by the war. The Prince of Wales's Fund had been set afoot, and the Queen lost no time in issuing an appeal to women, calling upon them to give their services and to aid in the local administration of the funds raised; and we on our part also lost no time in recommending our societies to offer all possible help by communicating with their Lord Mayors, Mayors, or Chairmen of the Local Councils, placing at their disposal the services of the Society. We felt the following forms of help would be greatly needed : the care of young women out of work, of whom at the outset of the war there were large numbers ; the care of foreigners stranded in this country (this work was presently taken over by our sister Society, the British Branch of the International Women's Suffrage Alliance) ; the offer of houses for use as con-valescent homes for men, women, and children. We also very early arrived at the conclusion that the care of infant life, saving the children, and protecting their welfare was as true a service to the country as that which men were rendering by going into the armies to serve in the field. The foundation of Infant Welfare Centres received a great impetus from our societies, and work on these lines had the further advantage, from our point of view, of not arousing antagonism from our Quaker members, always good fighters, who formed an important element in many of our societies. Preservation of food supplies and their economical use were of obvious importance. Activity on these lines found many zealous helpers, especially in the fruit-growing country of Hereford and Worcester. Leading members of our societies there took a very active part in saving the great fruit crops which were then hanging in the orchards and threatened by destruction in consequence of shortage

of labour : the saving of these supplemented the food
supply for the coming winter. I have in mind the work
of one of our members in the Pershore country who did
much to save, and teach others to save, their apples and
plums ; she also in the following year took round a
travelling kitchen to help the cottage women to lay down
stocks of bottled fruit for their children.

The Executive Committee presently laid down a
formula intended to cover all work of this kind and
encouraged the N.U.W.S. Societies to undertake any
work tending to "*sustain the vital energies of the nation
while the strain of the war lasted.*" We made no effort
to dictate to our societies what form of national work
they should undertake. There was, indeed, a very wide
choice. I, as President, had called upon all our societies
to aid our country to the utmost by devising and carrying
out well-thought-out plans of national usefulness. The
societies responded splendidly. Edinburgh, under the
leadership of Dr. Elsie Inglis, devised the sending
abroad of Hospital Units entirely officered by women,
which became known a little later as the Scottish Women's
Hospitals. This eventually became almost a world
movement. By October 1918 it was maintaining 1,885
beds and had raised for their maintenance by private
subscription the sum of £428,905. Dr. Elsie Inglis's
life has been written by Lady Frances Balfour, and
in this book may be gathered some idea of the inspiration
which she brought to her work. There was at first,
of course, no encouragement whatever given by the
Army Medical Department or the British Red Cross
to women's Hospital Units. At the beginning of September 1914, when Dr. Elsie sought an interview in
Scotland with the head of the R.A.M.C. there, she asked
his advice as to how she could best place her knowledge
and skill as a surgeon at the disposal of her country.
This wiseacre replied, " Dear lady, go home and keep

quiet." The British Red Cross adopted the same attitude, and when Dr. Louisa Garrett Anderson and Dr. Flora Murray, who belonged to the militant group, were ready in the first month of the war to take their hospital equipment and staff as near the front as they could, they also were refused any help or recognition. They, and also Dr. Inglis, were therefore compelled to place their organizations under the French Red Cross. The history of these Women's Hospitals marks an epoch in the history of the women's movement in England, France, and Serbia. In England there was soon a complete change of front on the part of Sir Alfred Keogh, the head of the R.A.M.C. in this country. With great generosity he said, after having seen the work of Dr. Murray and Dr. Anderson in their hospitals in Paris and Wimereux, that they were really worth their weight, not in gold, but in diamonds. In France, leading men of science, such as Dr. Weinberg, *chef de laboratoire* at the Pasteur Institute, Paris, paid an overwhelmingly favourable tribute to the scientific as well as to the medical and surgical work of the Scottish Women's Hospital at Royaumont, and with sound logic expressed the opinion that nothing could more effectively further the cause of the women's movement than the work he had investigated at this great hospital.[1] In Serbia the birth of the women's movement was simultaneous with the work done mainly by British women in saving the country from the destruction which was threatened by the terrible outbreak of typhus in 1915. Our other work in the meantime was progressing rapidly.

Our London Society, with its very able secretary, Miss Philippa Strachey, concentrated on sorting out

[1] See also *Women as Army Surgeons*, by Dr. Flora Murray; *The Scottish Women's Hospital*, by Mrs. Shaw MacLaren; and *The Scottish Women's Hospital at Royaumont*, by M. Antonio de Navarro; also brief references in Dr. Agnes Savill's book, *Music, Health and Character*, and in my own little book, *The Women's Victory and After*.

women who were seeking work to societies, Government offices, and individuals who needed them. They did this so successfully that they became an information bureau in all matters relating to women's employment and professional training, and since the war they still continue this most useful work. Quite early in the war they changed their name from the London Society for Women's Suffrage to the London Society for Women's Service. All our societies were soon working energetically and usefully and we were very successful when we asked the co-operation of societies outside our own organization. In the first autumn of the war the necessity of women's work in the training camps to which tens of thousands of young men were thronging was brought to the notice of the N.U.W.S.S. by one of our members, Mrs. Uniacke, the wife of an officer on active service. We agreed that the matter could best be dealt with by the National Council of Women. Mrs. Creighton was then president, and at our instance took up the work of instituting "Women Patrols" who in their turn led in a few years to the appointment of Women Police.

If I may be forgiven for referring to my own personal feelings, I may mention that the day on which we knew we were actually at war with the greatest military nation in the world was the most miserable of my life. I do not think I ever doubted that in the end we should win. The idea that Great Britain should ever really be crushed by the iron heel of German militarism never found a place in my mind : but so ill did I read the future that I thought the hope of women's freedom was indefinitely postponed, and that this was the supreme sacrifice asked of us at this stupendous moment. Black indeed the outlook seemed. The next overwhelmingly miserable day to me was Sunday, 23rd August, when terrible rumours reached London of the retreat from

Mons and the supposed destruction of our Expeditionary Force. I thought and thought of all those departed from this life whom I had most loved, and thanked God they were no longer here to endure the misery through which we were passing. It was some comfort when we heard that after all it was retreat and not destruction to which our men had been subjected. Nevertheless, the outlook could hardly have been worse ; the fortresses at Liége and Namur had fallen one after the other ; the Library at Louvain had been burnt ; Brussels was occupied ; untold, untellable horrors [1] were being per-petrated by the Germans in their victorious advance through Belgium; and now they were almost at the gates of Paris ; the French Government had departed to Bordeaux ; at home Lord Kitchener was warning us not to be elated by the crowds besieging the recruiting offices and training camps, for it would take fully three years to defeat the Germans ; our spirits were at a very low ebb.

Then on a quiet afternoon, the last Sunday in August, a taxi with luggage appeared at our door and a woman doctor, a Frau X., English by birth but married to a German and long resident in Germany and a naturalized German, deposited herself at our house. In happier days she had been our friend. She had come, she said, with a falsified passport to warn us—nay, to entreat us—to use such influence as we possessed to persuade the English people to submit at once and make terms before it was too late ; the Germans, she said, were absolutely invincible, to resist them was mere folly ; did not their present progress prove it ? Paris was bound to fall, and London would immediately follow ; the German Kaiser would fulfil his prophecy that he would ride triumphantly through London with the Crown Princess at his side, and eat his Christmas dinner in Buckingham

[1] See *Report of Lord Bryce's Committee*, 1915.

Palace. "You could save yourselves all this," she argued, "by submission now." As she talked we grew angrier and angrier. "They will drop their bombs from the skies and set fire to the town," she continued. We had had no experience of air-raids then, though we had plenty a little later. "Yes," we replied, "we know they will ; they will naturally aim at the British Museum "—the most prominent object from our windows—" and as they are not very good shots they will miss the Museum and hit us ; but that is just as it should be." Frau X. was a Social Democrat, and she declared solemnly that if Germany were successful in this war the Kaiser had intimated his intention of relaxing the extraordinary franchise laws of Prussia which virtually disfranchised all but a small fraction of the population. We retorted that his promises did not count for much if we could judge by his regard for his treaty obligations to respect the neutrality of Belgium.

At length, when we had thoroughly irritated each other, she began to take her leave ; the cab had been at the door all the time with her luggage upon it, and our impression was, and is, that she had contemplated taking up her abode under our roof. This we were determined she should not do. It would have been more than we could bear to have her domiciled in our house. When she was making her adieux, she said, "You will not, of course, give any information about my presence in England with a false passport." I replied that I could give no pledge whatever as to this. If it seemed in my judgment desirable, I should certainly give information to the authorities that she was in this country and had a passport which she told me was worthless. She was angry, but I could give her no satisfaction on this point. I never had occasion to act on my implied threat. She took up her abode first in one family and then in a second, and finally in a third, with all of whom I was well acquainted. I certainly wished her well out of the country, for she was frequently haunting our offices, and was there, in my opinion, for no good, as she was mainly bent on serving the purposes of her adopted country. Neither the Foreign Office nor Scotland Yard nor anyone in England seemed in the least anxious to get rid of her, and she remained in London a long time after she was panting to get back to Germany. The situation became rather ridiculous. The official view seemed to be that she was doing no harm here, and might as well remain. Our Secret Service Bureau was much more efficient than the Germans had expected, and there was probably little about Frau X. which they had to learn. As a matter of fact, all sorts of strings had to be pulled to obtain leave for her to depart. Poor woman, I wondered at the time whether she had been sent to England by the German Government, and I wondered still more when, about eighteen months later, another English woman doctor, who had been resident in Germany for some time, came to me on much the same errand. She also urged that Germany was invincible ; no one in Germany was suffering in the slightest degree from scarcity of the necessities and luxuries of life. She had just seen the Christmas shops full of all kinds of things which people were buying freely ; we had much better give in at once and get better terms than we should if we fought on to the bitter end. It would interest me to hear if other people had similar communications. There is a letter quoted in full in Mr. Walter H. Page's *Life and Letters*, vol. i, pages 347-51, from an English woman married to a German living in Bremen, which strengthens my suspicions that this was a deliberately planned official method of trying to break down the " Home Front " in this country. If so, it was singularly unsuccessful, like other cunning little dodges which some Germans considered so clever. The Bremen lady wrote :

" As to the future, you cannot win . . . the officers
of the neighbouring commands are absolutely certain
that they will land ten Army Corps in England before
Christmas. It is terrible to know what they mean to
go for. They mean to destroy. Every town which is
even remotely connected with war material is to be
annihilated. Birmingham, Bradford, Leeds, Newcastle,
Sheffield, Northampton are to be wiped out, the men
killed and ruthlessly hunted down. . . . Ireland will be
left independent, and its harmlessness will be guaranteed
by its inevitable civil war," and so on for two or three
large pages. It is curiously satisfactory to remember
how quietly England took all this. We had Esther's
saying in our hearts, " If we perish, we perish," but we
had no idea of giving in to this bluster and bullying.

Chapter XXIII

NATIONAL VICTORY AND SUFFRAGE VICTORY COME IN SIGHT

THERE WERE TWO POLITICAL EVENTS in the latter part of the Great War which in combination made the victory for Suffrage certain.

The first was the very great impression made throughout the country by the national value of women's war services and the ungrudging, unbargaining generosity of spirit with which they had been rendered.

The second was the extremely defective character of our old franchise law, which made it absolutely necessary to carry a Reform Bill through all its stages before the war ended. Dwelling first on the first of these, there was not a paper in Great Britain that by 1916-17 was not ringing with praise of the courage and devotion of British women in carrying out war work of various kinds, and on its highly effective character from the national point of view. The Prefect of Constanza was quoted as having said of the women orderlies of the Scottish Women's Hospital in Serbia, " It is extraordinary how these women endure hardships ; they refuse help and carry the wounded themselves. They work like navvies. No wonder England is a great country if the women are like that." Another story which moved the whole country was this : a ship coming from Australia, bringing troops and a group of women nurses, was torpedoed in the Mediterranean. The captain ordered the lifeboats out, and gave the usual order " Save the women first," but the nurses drew back and said, " Fighting men first ; they are the country's greatest need." Men could hardly speak of these things without tears in their eyes. The industrial women brought the same spirit to their work. They were out for what they could give and not for what they could get. Dame Adelaide Anderson, then Chief Woman Factory Inspector, wrote repeatedly in her reports of the wonderful and unsparing work of the industrial women everywhere, especially when they were working on Government orders for the supply of our fighting men. The Press was full of unmeasured praise for the efficiency of this work and the zeal with which it was performed ; the words " wonderful," " amazing," " extraordinary " were sprinkled over the articles and rather irritated some of us, to whom it seemed as if the writers had never before realized the skill and efficiency of women's pre-war work, whether in the home or in the factory. By special arrangements with the Trade Unions, women in 1915 were allowed to undertake industrial work hitherto closed to them. The relaxation of the Trade Union rules was temporary, and was thoroughly understood on both sides to be so. The first time I perceived what a factor this industrial freedom, temporary though it was, was going to become in our political work was when I read in the trade journal, *The Engineer,* in August 1915, quoted by Miss Lowndes in her valuable magazine, *The Englishwoman,* " that women were doing work in engineering requiring great skill and intelligence "—no mere routine work requiring only patience and endurance, but " work of which any skilled mechanic might be proud." Sir William Beardmore, the President of the Iron and Steel Institute, referred in his Presidential Address, 1915, to the high productiveness of women's labour. He spoke of a machine recently introduced by his firm of which they desired to test the utility. A good workman was induced, with some difficulty, to lay aside, for the sake of the experiment, the traditional restriction of output. The machine did well, but not so well as the firm had expected. Then a further experiment was made, and women were put on the job ; " using the same machine and working the same hours, their output was more than double that of the trained mechanic." Another case was often quoted—that of a former charwoman who had been put on to do gun-breech work. Her job was to bore a hole ⅛ of an inch in diameter dead true through 12 inches of solid steel. The test was the tally of broken tools, and at the time of writing, the reports said this woman, the former " char," had a clean slate.

When the women were put on munition work, every successive Minister of Munitions spoke enthusiastically of the value of what they were doing for the country. Mr. Lloyd George led off, and said their work was " indispensable and of extraordinary value. I am anxious," he said, " to bear testimony to the tremendous part played by the women of England in this vital epoch of human history." His successors, Mr. Montagu and Mr. Winston Churchill, were no less enthusiastic. One said, " It is not too much to say that our armies have been saved and victory assured by the women in the munition factories " ; while the other declared that " Without the work of women it would have been impossible to win the war," and also referred to its excellent quality as well as its enormous volume. Sir Lyndon Macassey, in a Quarterly article, said that " Where the work required constant alertness, a sure and deft touch, and delicacy of manipulation, women were invariably superior to men."[1] Evidence of this kind, piled up as it was day after day in the Press, brought about a very significant change in public opinion on the whole question of women's place in industry and in national life. Even the great Anti-

[1] *Quarterly Review,* July 1919, p. 81.

Suffrage fortress, manned by Mr. Asquith, and those to whom his light was a guiding star, showed signs of hanging out a flag of surrender. This was first noticed in October 1915, on the occasion of Mr. Asquith's comment in the House of Commons on the heroic death of Edith Cavell. Referring to what had happened during the fifteen months of war to justify faith in the manhood and womanhood of the country, he added, speaking of Miss Cavell, " She has taught the bravest man among us a supreme lesson of courage ; yes, and in this United Kingdom and throughout the Dominions there are thousands of such women, but *a year ago we did not know it.*" Pathetic blindness ! especially as a great deal of it must have been wilful.

Throughout the years 1916 and 1917 conversions of important public men and of leading newspapers kept coming in, not by ones and twos, but by battalions. The Anti-Suffrage Press, which in earlier days had been such an obstacle in the way of our success, was almost wiped out. The three Posts, as we called them, *The Morning Post, The Birmingham Post,* and the *Yorkshire Post,* alone remained obdurate, but after this two out of these three revised and modified their position. What a contrast to the time when a leading journal could write, " The female sex has nothing whatever to complain of ; its merits, where they exist, are fully recognized ; does not the epicure prefer the female herring ? " The wave of appreciation of women's work and place in the world rose higher and higher, and had permanent results ; the value of it is felt in many directions ; we see evidence of it in the greater courtesy extended to women everywhere ; in the greater appreciation of the value of infant life ; in the greater willingness of men to share in and help women in their domestic work. Instances will occur to almost everyone. I believe also that the institution of the Boy Scout and Girl

Guide movement was very helpful in the same direction. It was an inspiration to require from every Boy Scout that he should do at least one kind action every day.

I now come to the second contributory cause of our victory in 1917-18. We have not yet forgotten that under the old franchise law the names on the Parliamentary Register for the whole United Kingdom numbered roughly 8,000,000 ; of these, still quoting in round figures, 7,000,000 qualified as householders, and it was necessary for the occupier before he could get on the Register to show that he had been uninterruptedly in occupation of the qualifying premises for twelve months previous to the preceding 15th July. This meant, after the outbreak of the Great War, that the very men who had been most eager to join the Army and had given up everything to offer their services to their country had by that very act in numerous cases forfeited their qualification as voters. That this disfranchising result affected a very large number of the best men in the country cannot be doubted. By the end of the war Great Britain was maintaining in the field more than eight and a half million men ; of these, 7,000,000 were white men enlisted within the British Empire.[1] What was the exact proportion of those who had thereby lost their votes in Great Britain cannot be ascertained, but it must have been very considerable.

The Government quite early in the war had suspended the annual revision of the Parliamentary Register, and therefore there are no means of judging exactly what elements in the former electorate ceased to be qualified as voters, but when an occasional by-election had taken place it was found that the existing Register was so imperfect as to be practically useless. Candidates and agents reported the existence of street after street in which only a handful of voters remained. Under these

[1] See Report of War Cabinet Committee published in August 1918.

circumstances Mr. Asquith had declared that a Parliament elected on such a Register would be "lacking in moral sanction." In 1915 another political change had taken place which materially strengthened our prospects of success : a minor Ministerial crisis occurred during the spring, and a Coalition Government had been formed. This necessitated the recasting of the whole Government and Cabinet, and resulted, with one or two notable exceptions, in the removal of men in the old Liberal administration who were our inveterate enemies, and the substitution of men who had long been convinced and devoted supporters of women's enfranchisement. I will not dwell on the names of those who "came out," but among those who "came in" were Lord Robert Cecil (now Lord Cecil of Chelwood), Lord Selborne, representing the Conservatives, and Mr. Henderson, representing Labour. This obviously strengthened the Suffrage party in the Government. Sir John Simon, whose work for us later was of great importance, was promoted from being a law officer to be Secretary of State for the Home Department. On the other hand, however, we lost Lord Haldane, who up to 1915 had been Lord Chancellor and in all respects a thorough and trustworthy friend of our cause. I always felt that he had been very unjustly thrown to the wolves of a newspaper stunt. When, therefore, the necessity of passing a great Reform Bill during the war was more and more recognized, our chances of having women included in it were greatly improved. Still, we believed we had to reckon with the continued opposition of the Prime Minister, Mr. Asquith, a past-master of the manipulation of the Parliamentary machine, who would use all his arts and crafts against us. In 1916, therefore, the National Union of Women's Suffrage Societies addressed to him the following letter. It will be readily believed that we discussed every sentence of it before it was finally agreed upon.

4*th May* 1916.

DEAR MR. ASQUITH,

I am venturing once more to address you on the subject of the enfranchisement of women.

A very general rumour has prevailed since last autumn, supported by statements made by responsible persons and by its own inherent reasonableness, that the Government will, before the General Election following the end of the war, find it necessary to deal with the franchise question in order to prevent the hardship and injustice which would arise if men who have been serving their country abroad, or in munition areas in parts of the country other than those where they usually reside, should in consequence of their patriotic service be penalized by losing their votes.

This has caused a certain amount of restlessness and anxiety among the 500 or 600 societies forming the N.U.W.S.S., as well as among other Suffrage organizations. Not, of course, that any of us are in any degree hostile to the enfranchisement of men who have been suffering and working for our country, but it is feared that the Suffrage may be dealt with in a manner prejudicial to the future prospects of the enfranchisement of women. To allay this feeling of restlessness and anxiety, we desire to bring certain considerations before you and to ask you for an expression of your opinion upon them.

When the Government deals with the franchise an opportunity will present itself of dealing with it on wider lines than by the simple removal of what may be called the accidental disqualification of a large body of the best men in the country, and we trust that you may include in your Bill clauses which would remove the disabilities under which women now labour. An agreed Bill on these lines would, we are confident, receive a very wide measure of support throughout the country. Our movement has received very great accessions of strength during recent months, former opponents now declaring themselves on our side, or, at any rate, withdrawing their opposition. The change of tone in the Press is most marked.

These changes are mainly consequent on the changed industrial and professional status of women, and the view has been widely expressed in a great variety of organs of public opinion that the continued exclusion of women from representation will, on these grounds, be an impossibility after the war.

If I refer to what the N.U.W.S.S. has done in the way of service to the country since the war began, it is not that I claim for it any greater degree of patriotism than has been shown practically by all women. I only mention it because I can speak with personal knowledge of it. Within two days of the declaration of war, the N.U.W.S.S. determined to suspend its ordinary political activities, and to devote its organization and money-raising powers to alleviate distress arising out of the war, and to other work calculated to sustain, as far as might be, the vital energies of the nation during the great struggle which lay before it.

In this work we have had a considerable measure of success, but I will not trouble you with any detailed recital of it. We know from our own experience, and we trust that you also realize, that women of all classes are eager to bear their full share of the work and the suffering demanded from the country, and that wherever opportunity has been given them they have devoted themselves with whole-hearted eagerness to the national work they have found to do. The record of our own Scottish Women's Hospitals bears proof of this fact, which is now widely recognized throughout the world.

We believe that it is the recognition of the active, self-sacrificing, and efficient national service of women which has caused the recent access of strength to the movement we represent.

We should greatly value an expression of your views upon the subject of the possibility of the Government dealing with the franchise question in the direction indicated above.

Believe me, dear Mr. Asquith,

Yours very faithfully,

MILLICENT GARRETT FAWCETT.

On behalf of the National Union of Women's Suffrage Societies.

Mr. Asquith's reply ran as follows :

10, DOWNING STREET, S.W.,
7th May 1916.

DEAR MRS. FAWCETT,

I have received your letter of the 4th. I need not assure you how deeply my colleagues and I recognize and appreciate the magnificent contribution which the women of the United Kingdom have made to our country's cause.

No such legislation as you refer to is at present in contemplation ; but if, and when, it should become necessary to undertake it you may be certain that the considerations set out in your letter will be fully and impartially weighed without any pre-judgment from the controversies of the past.

Yours very faithfully,

H. H. ASQUITH.

Although Mr. Asquith said in this letter that no such legislation was " at present in contemplation "—that is, on 7th May 1916—it was very soon in contemplation and was the subject in a few weeks of repeated debates and questions asked and answered in Parliament.

Mr. Asquith for a considerable time entertained the idea, and endeavoured to induce the House of Commons to entertain it, that the situation created by the breakdown of our electoral system could be dealt with by a mere tinkering with the Register : the Government therefore began a series of futile attempts to persuade the House to adopt a " Special Register " Bill. Sir Edward (now Lord) Carson was at the same time pressing for a new franchise giving the vote to sailors, soldiers, and airmen as such, on the ground of their war services. Our friends retorted " had not women given war services, too ? " and the Press comment generally was that the Bill could not include soldiers and exclude women. In the meantime, soldiers themselves were giving indications that they had no wish to exclude women. In Canada, Women's Suffrage and women's eligibility had been granted a little in advance of our victory in Great Britain. A General Election was held, and under Canadian law the election for the province of Alberta was practically in the hands of 38,000 soldiers and 75 Army nurses, then serving in France. There were twenty men candidates and one woman, Miss R. C. MacAdams. Before the war, Miss MacAdams had been a science teacher in the Alberta public schools, and had held other important educational posts : at the time of the election she was working as a nurse in the military hospital at Orpington, Kent. Her election address was simple and to the point : reconstruction would, she said, be the main duty of the new Parliament, when the war was over; and she held that while men were apt to think in terms of territory, money, and material wealth, women were apt to think in terms of human life. She did not claim that either of these terms should be neglected, but it was surely desirable that the more human aspect of economic and political questions should be considered. She was elected on the soldiers' vote. This was another great encouragement to us. Moreover, I was told by one of our fighting men, who was also a Member of Parliament, that when with the Army in France he had had a letter from Mr. Arnold Ward, then acting as Whip to the Anti-Suffragists in the House of Commons, begging my informant to come over and vote against Women's Suffrage in important divisions which were in prospect. The reply was that if he came at all he should vote for and not against the enfranchisement of women. I thought of the time when Mr. (afterwards Lord) Bryce, speaking against us in the House of Commons some fifteen years earlier, had said that Women's Suffrage was an untried experiment. " It is a very bold experiment," he said ; " our Colonies are democratic in the highest degree, why do they not try it ? " This was followed almost at once by the adoption of Women's Suffrage in New Zealand and South Australia : it was also adopted by the Commonwealth of Australia as soon as the States resolved to form themselves into a Union, and by all the separate States in turn.

The diminishing ranks of the Anti-Suffragists in England had seemed to assume as a matter of course that our fighting men, then actually in the field, would be unanimous against allowing women any direct influence in political affairs. They discovered that they were wholly wrong. War was a great revealer of the reality of things. Shams and subterfuges withered in its great glare, and the men subjected to it saw men and women and the real and false values of life as they actually were. There was a tide in the affairs of men, a great wave, a wave of vitality which seemed to inspire men and women to live greatly and to do nobly. It was a tide which moved men ; it was not moved by them.

It was in the House of Commons on 14th August 1916 that Mr. Asquith had the courage to confess his former errors. If he had discovered his mistake fifteen or twenty years sooner, we should have been saved from militancy with all its heartbreaking suffering and squalid incidents : for he was responsible for having

led a large section of his party astray on our question :
but of course the penitent was not to be rebuffed although
the harm he had done before his repentance was difficult
to measure. His reasons for his change of view were
stated in the House, needless to say, with dignity and
force. His support had been in part won by the war
service of women, but what had made a special appeal
to him had been the fact that when

these abnormal and, of course, to a large extent transient conditions
have to be revised and when the process of industrial reconstruction has
to be set on foot, the House will agree that the women have a special
claim to be heard on the many questions which will arise directly affecting
their interests, and possibly meaning for them large displacements of
labour ? I cannot think that the House will deny, and I say quite
frankly that I cannot deny, that claim.

Now that the Prime Minister had discovered a ladder
down which he could climb in renunciation of his former
errors, the next step in the art of Parliamentary government was to devise other ropes and routes down which
other M.P.'s could make their descent safely and with
dignity. The device adopted was the appointment of
what was known as the Speaker's Conference, non-party
in character, consisting entirely of members of the
two Houses of Parliament, nominated and presided over
by the then Speaker, Mr. Lowther (now Lord Ullswater).
He was an Anti-Suffragist himself, but was justly famed
for his power of holding the balance even between
contending factions, and also for courtesy and humour,
always a great solvent of difficulties. The questions
referred to the Conference included the whole subject
of electoral reform, such as votes for soldiers and sailors
as such, Proportional Representation, adult suffrage,
plural voting, and also votes for women. The question of women's votes was not emphasized in any way
at the time when the Conference was agreed to by Parliament, but there can be little doubt that it provided
the main motive power which led to its appointment.

The House of Commons had got almost out of hand, and quite out of temper over Mr. Asquith's attempts to show that the difficulties inherent in the situation could be dealt with by a Registration Bill : but of course he elaborated the subject with all the art of the accomplished Parliamentarian, and presently propounded the plan of first submitting the whole difficulty to the judgment of the House of Commons itself. He wrapped this up so skilfully that his words made it appear that to leave this important decision to the House was a positive compliment to its sagacity : but one of his followers, less versed in the arts of government than himself, had charge of the matter a few days later, and said bluntly that it was because the difficulty under consideration was insoluble that its solution was left to the House. He set forth all the difficulties. Something had got to be done : the old Register was useless, a new Register on the old basis was nearly as bad, as it would still disfranchise our fighting men, and then the House would have to take up the difficult controversial questions of Women's Suffrage, plural voting, adult suffrage, etc. This caused a genuine blaze of rage in the House : the Cabinet had thrown the problem to the House, and the House threw it back to the Cabinet, who were told, not too politely, to do their own job. Then followed another protracted period of consideration and hesitation : the Speaker's Conference solution finally emerged. During the preliminary discussions in Parliament and in the Speaker's Conference itself, our cause received invaluable services from Sir John Simon. Details concerning this and also concerning the splendid help we received at every critical moment from Lord Robert Cecil, Sir W. H. Dickinson, and Mr. Bonar Law can be found in my little book, *The Women's Victory and After*, already referred to.

In the Cabinet itself, we were told, on good authority, that our chief friends had been Lord Robert Cecil, Mr.

Lloyd George, and Mr. Arthur Henderson, who fought our battles for us again and again. This was particularly satisfactory to us as a non-party association, because the three friends just named belonged respectively to the Conservative, the Liberal, and the Labour Party.

When Mr. Asquith ceased to be Prime Minister in December 1916 he was succeeded by Mr. Lloyd George. Lord Northcliffe, who had been in the earlier years of our movement one of its opponents, had now become its ardent supporter. He had watched with a trained and skilful eye its growing strength and volume, and became convinced that the change in the Premiership, from the hands of a skilful and dexterous enemy to those of an equally dexterous and skilful friend, made the moment particularly propitious for a big step in advance. He wrote to Lady Betty Balfour on the subject, and his letter began with the words " *There is absolutely no movement anywhere for Women's Suffrage.*" He then suggested that she should get up a large meeting or a demonstration in its support. Lady Betty forwarded this letter to me. It made me very angry, and I wrote back in a white heat to Lady Betty. I have not any draft of my letter, but I know that I recounted how from the beginning of the war we had suspended all our political work, and had concentrated our organizing and money-raising power on various services to our country. I mentioned the Scottish Women's Hospitals, with funds bordering on half a million sterling, raised in all parts of the British Empire, and maintaining 1,800 beds : our Hospital Units sent to Russia to help the civil population there : our work for our soldiers in the training camps all over the kingdom : the recognition of the value of British women's work by our Allies in France and Serbia, as well as by the head of the R.A.M.C. in our own country, and so on : and yet, because we broke no windows and attempted no injury to anyone, Lord Northcliffe declared that "there was absolutely no movement for Women's Suffrage anywhere." I had no patience with people who could see nothing unless their heads were broken with it. Lord Northcliffe's whole attitude was absolutely unreasonable, and so on. Lady Betty sent my tirade on to Lord Northcliffe, and he then wrote to me direct, as follows :

Christmas Day, 1916.

DEAR MRS. FAWCETT,

I hope you will allow me to waive ceremony and defend my " unreasonable " sex against your attacks.

I do not suggest window-breaking, but I do think some great meeting or united deputation is necessary.

Public psychology is such that people can only think of one thing at a time. They are now thinking only of the war, and it is quite possible that legislation will arrive unnoticed that may be detrimental to the interests, not only of women, but to many other sections of the community.

Lady Betty has asked me to speak to the Prime Minister, and I will do so to-morrow.

Yours sincerely,

NORTHCLIFFE.

I wrote at once, thanking him for his advice, and explained that I could take no action without consulting with the officers of the N.U.W.S.S., but I was to meet them the next Friday morning, when we should very carefully consider his letter, and added :

I believe that as a consequence of the experience of the last twenty-nine months, Women's Suffrage has obtained a new and far stronger position than ever before ; and that this is due not only to the good work done by women, but to the good spirit in which it has been done, the spirit of whole-hearted love of our country and reverence for its aims in this war. It is this, if I mistake not, which has made such an impression on the public mind. We must beware of acting in any way calculated to weaken this impression, and from this point of view I incline to the big deputation rather than to the public meeting.

Yours sincerely,

M. G. FAWCETT.

In a further letter to Lady Betty, Lord Northcliffe said that he was going to read my letter, the fierce and angry one of which I have no copy, "*at* the Prime Minister to-morrow." So I felt I had done well to be angry. My next letter from Lord Northcliffe is characteristic. It was dated 27th December 1916 :

DEAR MRS. FAWCETT,

   I talked for some time last night with the Prime Minister, who is very keen on the subject and very practical, too. I make the suggestion to you and Lady Betty that you get up a large and representative deputation. That will give the newspapers the opportunity of dealing with the matter.

   I shall speak to the Editor of *The Times* on the question to-day. I believe he is entirely favourable.*

Yours sincerely,
NORTHCLIFFE.

   * " Have done so. He is."

Lord Northcliffe's support was of great value to our movement. He was constantly talking to his friends on our subject. He, who had been a few years earlier one of our chief opponents in the Press, was now reported to have said, " The women were wonderful. Their freshness of mind, their organizing skill, were magnificent. Men were making too great a mess of the world, and needed helpers without their own prejudices, idleness, and self-indulgence.[1]

We did not agree with Lord Northcliffe's diatribes against his own sex, but we welcomed his support as an indication of the great change in public opinion. From this time onward we made steady and rapid progress. In January 1917 the Report of the Speaker's Conference was published. It recommended that some measure of Women's Suffrage should be conferred, and also that it should be based on the Local Government Register with the very important addition of including the names of women whose husbands were on that Register, but that the age limit for women should be considerably higher than that for men. Eventually

   [1] This was kindly communicated to me by the late Mr. Massingham, then editor of *The Nation*.

the age limit for women was fixed at 30, while for men it remained 21, although boys even as young as 18 were allowed to vote if they had actually been in the fighting services. The high age limit for women was accepted by our friends in the Conference, because they believed that to insist on absolute equality would imperil our cause and might for the time be even fatal to it. The recommendation of Women's Franchise by the Speaker's Conference was welcomed with scarcely an exception by the Press of the country. It soon became apparent that the measures of enfranchisement recommended would, if adopted by Parliament, result in by far the largest number of votes being added to the Register that had ever been authorized by any previous Reform Bill. Our friends on the Speaker's Conference had aimed at a constituency in which the proportion of women to men in the new electorate would be two to three. This anticipation proved very nearly correct, for the new Register published in 1919 gave the number of men voters as 12,913,000 and the number of women voters as 8,470,150. We now found ourselves in the unprecedented position of receiving praise on all sides. Dear old Dr. Clifford, who had been our friend throughout, preached a sermon about us in which he said, among other things, " Opponents have changed into advocates with a suddenness that shows that winds of the spirit of Liberty have swept their minds clear of traditional prejudice and made them ready for a welcome. Think of it : a few years ago a few solitary voices like John Stuart Mill's exposed and denounced the ' subjection of women,' a few women like Mrs. Fawcett agitated for the Suffrage. Then came the revolt, violent, vehement, and desperate, of a few more, and now the war has placed their cause in such a position that it can never be put back. British women must be enfranchised."

From the dawn of 1917 until 16th February 1918,

when the new Reform Bill received the Royal Assent, so far as our work for women's citizenship was concerned it was " Roses, roses all the way " without the dismal sequel which Browning's hero had experienced. We hurried up with the organization of the deputation which Lord Northcliffe had recommended " to give the papers something to write about." The organization of this deputation was in the able hands of Mrs. O. Strachey— she made it picturesque as well as representative of the National Services given by women during the war, but it was really unnecessary ; we were pushing against an open door.

As there has been quite recently (1924) some controversy on the subject, I wish to make it plain that we never relinquished our full demand, " Suffrage for women on the same terms as it is, or may be, granted to men." As soon as the Report of the Speaker's Conference was in our hands I, as President of the N.U.W.S.S., wrote in our paper, *The Common Cause* [1] (now *The Woman's Leader*) that if anyone asked me if I were entirely satisfied by the proposals embodied in the Report I should answer by a distinct negative, and I continued, " We are asking, and shall continue to ask, for the Suffrage for women on the same terms as it is, or may be, granted to men. But I do not think it is very wonderful if, at one stroke, Parliament should refuse to enfranchise the whole female population. Men in this country have never been enfranchised in this whole-sale fashion."

Notwithstanding its superfluous character, our deputation to Mr. Lloyd George on 29th March was a very agreeable function. It was representative of the whole Suffrage movement. I had to explain that our original intention had been to ask the Prime Minister to introduce without delay legislation embodying the recommendation

[1] See *The Common Cause*, 9th February 1917.

of the Speaker's Conference, but as I had learned from his own speech, made two days earlier, that such legislation was already being framed, I contented myself with adding that if the Prime Minister should see his way when the Bill was in Committee to improve in a democratic direction upon the recommendations of the Conference—but only so far as was consistent with the safety of the whole scheme—I and Suffragists generally would be very gratified. I added on my own account that personally I greatly preferred an imperfect Bill, which could be passed, to the most perfect scheme in the world which could not pass.

In order to make the deputation more agreeable to the Prime Minister, Mrs. O. Strachey had had the happy thought of bringing a Welsh-speaking lady with us. What she said and what Mr. Lloyd George replied remained unknown to us, but we believe it was something very agreeable and pleasant, judging by the expression on the faces of the two Welsh scholars. Before we left I told Mr. Lloyd George that it was only through an accident that Miss Violet Markham had not joined us, and the Prime Minister exclaimed, " Miss Markham a convert ! This is welcome news indeed."

It is unnecessary to go through the details of the victories for the women's cause signalized by the size of our majorities when the Reform Bill was in the House of Commons. But it came to our knowledge afterwards that it was the overwhelming character of the majorities in the Commons that gave us deep water enough to float our measure over the rocks of the House of Lords. In the Commons the second reading of the Bill was carried by 329 to 40, and when Committee was reached the division on the clause which enfranchised women resulted in giving 385 votes in our favour to 55 against, or exactly 7 to 1, *with a majority within each party into which the House was divided*. The leaders of each of these parties supported us by speech in the House Mr. Asquith, the most persistent and most effective of our former opponents, had just moved a resolution in the House, calling upon the Government to produce a Bill founded upon the recommendations of the Conference. He had confessed his errors and had likened himself to Stesichorus, who had been smitten with blindness for insulting Helen of Troy. He added, " Some of my friends may think that, like him, my eyes which for years in this matter have been clouded by fallacies and sealed by illusions, at last have been opened to the truth." I sometimes smile to myself when I remember these things, and also when I remember the French proverb, " Plus cela change, plus c'est la même chose." The prejudices of a lifetime may bow to the inevitable, but it takes more than a Parliamentary majority to entirely uproot them.

The immense majorities by which the women's clauses of the Reform Bill had been carried in the Commons had encouraged us to press for the application to the Local Government Register of the principles already accepted by the House in regard to the Parliamentary Franchise, i.e. to give the vote not only to women who were already entitled to be on the Local Government Register, but also to the wives of the men who were upon it. We obviously had a strong case for urging this, and we approached Ministers on the subject with confidence, but found them obdurate. Then we turned on the tap of electoral pressure and urged our many hundreds of societies all over the country to take up the matter with their own members, and also with the Minister concerned. This they did, with the result that the President of the Local Government Board was snowed under with letters and telegrams urging that the principle adopted for the extension of the Parliamentary vote to women should also apply to local elections. We were almost startled by our success. We were not then so accustomed as we have since become to the greater weight given to protests and resolutions when they proceed from voters. The Minister in charge, Mr. W. Long (afterwards Lord Long) gave way. He said he had received almost innumerable letters and telegrams all urging one thing, and not a single communication on the other side, and he agreed to apply to the Local Government Register the principles already adopted for the Parliamentary vote. Miss Rathbone was our leader in this part of our work. I was at first rather timid and feared to risk a setback in our main work ; but I was wrong, and the enormous extension given to the representation of women in Local Government has worked extraordinarily well, and did not at all injure any other branch of our activities.

The victory in the Commons was complete and sweeping, and the next question was how should we fare in the Lords ? We had great and important friends there : Lord Selborne, Lord Lytton, Lord Courtney, Lord Morley, Lord Burnham, Lord Buckmaster, Lord Milner, Lord Haldane, the Archbishops of Canterbury and York, and most of the Bishops. But we had great and important enemies also : Lord Bryce, Lord Lansdowne, Lord Balfour of Burleigh, and more powerful than all, Lord Curzon, who represented the Government in the House, and was therefore its leader and moreover was the President of the Anti-Suffrage League. As the debate proceeded it was impossible to feel any certainty as to how the voting would go. It all depended on Lord Curzon and what he said as the leader of the House. Mrs. Strachey and I had been so fortunate as to secure seats in the very small space allotted to ladies, other than peeresses, in the House. About eight of us were packed into a small pewlike enclosure level with the floor of the House. My next neighbour on one side was Mrs. Oliver Strachey and on the other Mrs. Humphry Ward.

Mr. Arnold Ward, M.P., her son, stood at the bar and was in frequent communication with his mother. The excitement was intense ; the debate on this one clause had lasted over two days, and now a decisive vote was about to be taken. In one of our snatches of conversation, Mrs. Humphry Ward had asked me, " in the event, which I do not anticipate, of the view I take being unsuccessful," would I support her in an agitation for the Referendum ? I replied at once in the negative, and said I had no affection for the Referendum, and believed it was an instrument of government most respected when it was least known. I had made, I told her, at one time a collection of the sayings of members of a former Government about the Referendum. One had called it " an expensive way of denying justice," while another described it as " just the thing for female suffrage." But, of course, while Lord Curzon was speaking our whole attention was centred on him ; at first fears and then hopes prevailed. He began with a skilful, but not at all original, Anti-Suffrage speech. He quoted, I am glad to recall now, a resolution recently adopted by the N.U.W.S.S. stating plainly that even if the Bill then before the House went through and became law, the N.U. would, of course, continue to work for suffrage for women on the same terms as for men. (Sir William Bull and Lord Eustace Percy, please note.) Continuing the discussion on Anti-Suffrage lines for a considerable time, he paused and asked the House to consider the subject carefully from another point of view—what would happen if they put themselves in opposition to the House of Commons on this matter within a few weeks of the other House having given a very large majority in favour of women's votes ? And he continued :

Your Lordships can vote as you please. You can cut this clause out of the Bill. You have a perfect right to do so. But if you think that by killing the clause you can also save the Bill, I believe you to be mistaken.

MILLICENT GARRETT FAWCETT IN 1918.

From a photograph

To face page 246

Nothing to my mind is more certain . . . than if your Lordships cut this clause out of the Bill, as you may perhaps be going to do, the House of Commons will return the Bill to you with the clause re-inserted. Will you be prepared to put it back ? Will you be content if you eliminate the clause with this vigorous protest that you have made, or will you be prepared to give way ? Or, if you do not give way, are you prepared to embark upon a conflict with a majority of 350 in the House of Commons, of whom nearly 150 belong to the party to which most of your Lordships belong ? . . . Therefore, my Lords, I cannot vote either this way upon the amendment, for I am loth to assume the responsibility of embarking upon a course which I might not be able to pursue and as regards which I might be accused of having precipitated a conflict from which your Lordships would not emerge with credit.[1]

These words made our victory in the Lords a certainty. It was, I think, the greatest moment of my life. We had won fairly and squarely after a fight lasting just fifty years. Henceforth, women would be free citizens. I spoke to Lord Aberconway, son of our valiant old friend Mrs. MacLaren, of Edinburgh, who happened to be standing near me at the bar, and asked what majority he thought we should have. He replied, " At least thirty." The numbers actually were : For the clause 134, against it 71, or nearly two to one. It was a complete and triumphant victory ; only twelve Anti-Suffrage peers followed Lord Curzon's example and abstained from voting, so that if they had all voted against us we should still have won. The Royal Assent was given by deputy in the House of Lords on 6th February 1918, a gorgeous ceremony which I had the pleasure of witnessing.

I was sorry for Mrs. Humphry Ward. She had always been an honourable opponent and had restrained her followers when they were trying to hit below the belt. But she was intensely indignant with Lord Curzon for his part in the debate, and burst out in uncontrollable rage against him, quoting Browning's " Lost Leader," and other similar things. He was correspondingly angry with her, and the quarrel found expression in the

[1] See *Hansard*, House of Lords, 10th January 1918, vol. xxvii, No. 108.

Morning Post 14th to 21st January 1918. She accused
Lord Curzon of keeping her in ignorance of the line
he intended to pursue, and he, replying, said that he had
given full information on this point to two members of
her committee before Christmas, and also to her son,
Mr. Arnold Ward, three weeks before the debate and
division had taken place. Why none of these had passed
on their information to Mrs. Ward, who was really their
leader and chief, has not been explained, so far as I know.
She certainly had a right to be angry with her colleagues
for keeping her in the dark. The correspondence in
the *Morning Post* ended with a letter from Mrs. Ward,[1]
conceived in a milder tone, and concluding, I am
glad to remember, with a friendly reference to myself.
"Amid my own disappointment," she wrote, " I could
not help thinking of Mrs. Fawcett, who had been
sitting beside me in the House of Lords, and feeling a
sort of vicarious satisfaction that after her long fight
she at least had gone home content." It was generously
said, and when the end of her life came suddenly about
two years later, I was glad to think of her words.

[1] On 3rd October 1924, Miss Dorothy Ward wrote to *The Woman's Leader*
that I was mistaken in assuming that Mrs. Ward had been kept in ignorance—
that the whole Anti-Suffrage Committee, including Mrs. Ward, knew beforehand that Lord Curzon would speak against, but not vote against, the Women's
clause of the Reform Bill : what they were not prepared for was the advice he
gave the Peers (quoted on the previous page) not to reject the clause. I accept
Miss Ward's correction as conclusive, but I hope I may be excused for the
error into which I have fallen ; what I relied on for my statement were a few
sentences in a letter from Mrs. Ward herself to the *Morning Post*, published
immediately after the division, 14th January 1918. Speaking of active communications having taken place between the Anti-Suffrage League and Lord
Curzon during the weeks immediately preceding the division, Mrs. Ward
stated in a conspicuous paragraph and without qualification *" We had no
reason to suppose that he [Lord Curzon] would take the line of action he did take.
No warning of any kind was given us."*

Chapter XXIV

CELEBRATING OUR VICTORY

W^{E HAD HELD} no great meetings in support of Women's Suffrage during the Great War, for we were then concentrating on various activities, calculated, as we hoped, to bring the war to a victorious conclusion. But in March 1918 we felt we must have one meeting of thanksgiving for the Parliamentary victory we had gained. This was fixed for the 13th March. Our desire was to assemble as many as possible of those who had been working for long years for the success of our cause, and to select our speakers from among the Members of Parliament who had effectively promoted it during the recent crisis which had ended in giving the franchise to about 8,000,000 women. I have already mentioned that our information was that the three men who had really won our cause for us in the Cabinet had been Mr. Lloyd George, Lord Robert Cecil, and Mr. Arthur Henderson. We did not succeed in getting all three, but among those who accepted our invitation to speak was Mr. Henderson, and it will be readily understood that I did not receive with any favour a protest from a " militant " clergyman of a City church against allowing him to appear on our platform. I supposed this to be a sort of echo of the futile Suffragette attempt in February 1914 to prevent Mr. Henderson from speaking for us. But my clerical friend was so persistent that at last I had to tell him plainly that the proposed meeting was ours, not his, and therefore the choice of speakers rested entirely with us. No repetition of the scene of 1914 was attempted. The meeting was equally harmonious and enthusiastic, and we were glad to receive messages of congratulation and good will from a large number of distinguished men and women, and also from a considerable proportion of old colleagues who had left us and set up a Society of their own in 1915.

Years before victory was in sight I had been accustomed to talk with my dear friend the late Mrs. Arthur Lyttelton about the best way of celebrating our triumph when it came. We had agreed that music alone could really convey what we should feel. Kathleen Lyttelton did not live to see our victory, but she and I had agreed that we must certainly have the Leonora Overture No. III, with its glorious burst of triumph when freedom displaces captivity and the overwhelming power of love overcomes the world of darkness. We had also hoped to have the last movement of Beethoven's Fifth Symphony, but that part of our dream never came true : there were difficulties we had not foreseen. But our friends among the great musicians came splendidly to our help. Chief of them was Sir Hubert Parry. He was ready to be our conductor. We had for some years been using Blake's noble poem " Jerusalem " as our Suffrage hymn. But there was no adequate music for it that matched in any sense with Blake's magical words, so we took this trouble to him, and asked him boldly to do the almost impossible, which he had done in his setting of Milton's " Blest Pair of Sirens." He most graciously promised to do what we asked of him, and the result was his splendid setting of Blake's poem, which is now known and sung wherever fine music and glorious words are wedded. Its first performance was at our Queen's Hall meeting in March 1918. I had the joy of hearing it every evening during the Leith Hill musical festival at Dorking in 1924, and no one but myself and a few friends knew that the music had been composed at our request. This same hymn was also a very marked feature of the Children's Day at Wembley on 24th May 1924.

> And did those feet in ancient times
> Walk upon England's mountains green?
> And was the Holy Lamb of God
> On England's pleasant pastures seen?
>
> And did the Countenance Divine
> Shine forth upon our clouded hills?
> And was Jerusalem builded here
> Among these dark Satanic mills?
>
> Bring me my bow of burning gold!
> Bring me my arrows of desire!
> Bring me my spear: O clouds unfold!
> Bring me my chariot of fire.
>
> I will not cease from mental fight,
> Nor shall my sword sleep in my hand,
> Till we have built Jerusalem
> In England's green and pleasant land.

Sir Hubert Parry was not the only great musician who befriended us and helped us with the musical part of our meeting. Mr. (now Sir Hugh) Allen, then Professor of Music at Oxford, made repeated journeys to and from London for the rehearsals ; he often returned to Oxford in the middle of the night or in the early hours of the morning and was undaunted either by the severe cold of an inclement spring or by the attentions of Zeppelins which from time to time held up his train. He was resolved to get the very best out of the orchestra, and I was told he would sometimes address them thus : " Of course you are all Suffragists, and will play your best for love of Suffrage ; but if there are two or three who are not Suffragists they will play their best for love of me."

We were very happy, and had cause to be. Things worked out even better and more rapidly than we had expected, though I had never had a moment's doubt of the final issue. When I was speaking almost perpetually all over the country in support of representative government and how it should include women, I was frequently asked if what the Suffrage Societies were aiming at was not " really and truly " to get women into Parliament. I said "No," the Suffrage Societies had but one aim, the vote for women on the same terms on which it was granted to men. The question of women in Parliament was one for constituencies to decide, and I cited the case of Jews in Parliament as an instance in point. I had not at all expected that the eligibility of women would follow as a matter of course immediately upon their enfranchisement. But this was the case ; women had been on the Parliamentary Register only a few months before the House of Commons decided, without any outside pressure, that they ought also to be entitled to sit as members. The necessary legislation to effect this, however, did not get through both Houses until just three weeks before the Dissolution of December 1918. It is not, therefore, very wonderful that no women were elected in that year; the wonder is that so many as sixteen were candidates. But 1919 saw the election of Viscountess Astor, who held the fort for us quite alone with a Joan of Arc gaiety and courage for which we can never be sufficiently grateful. Now, as everyone knows, she has seven women colleagues in the House, and the position is no longer so lonely and difficult.

Chapter XXV

POSTSCRIPT—PARIS IN 1919

WHEN THE SUFFRAGE BATTLE had been won in our own country in 1918, through the united efforts of hundreds of thousands of gallant comrades, men and women of all parties and all ranks, I felt I was justified in retiring from active work and in leaving the further development of our freedom in the able hands of my younger colleagues.

I have kept in close touch with many of them, and though I have freed myself from the burden of perpetual attendance at Committees, I have been ready to lend a hand when any piece of work came along which had grown out of our victory in 1918. Such was the call of French and American Suffragists in 1919, who felt that the Peace Congress in Paris was developing on lines which gave very scant consideration to the special needs and responsibilities of women. They therefore requested the presence in Paris of Suffragists of the Allied nations not in order to press with as much weight as possible for the enfranchisement of women in those countries which had not already achieved it, but for a consideration of even more fundamental issues such as, for instance, the infamous traffic in women and children usually called the White Slave Trade.

A group of ardent American women were already in Paris, and they united with French Suffragists, including Mme. de Witt Schlumberger, Mme. Avril de

Sainte Croix, Mme. Siegfried, and Mme. Thuillier Landry, in inviting an informal conference of women from all the Allied nations. The National Union of Women's Suffrage Societies having accepted this invitation, Mrs. Oliver Strachey, Miss Rosamund Smith, and myself were appointed as its representatives, and we were accompanied by a delightful New Zealand lady, Miss Atkinson, then visiting London and very proud of the fact that New Zealand had been the first independent country (in 1893) to give equal suffrage to women.

President Wilson had been extremely helpful to this project from the outset. He had replied to the deputations which had waited on him in January, "All I can do of course shall be done. I only hope you took my answer for granted."

When we arrived in Paris we were joined by representative Suffragists from Belgium and Italy besides, of course, those of America and France who had originated the conference.

Our first interview was with President Wilson, who gave us every encouragement and advised us to see as many as possible of the leaders of the Allied nations. Accordingly, during the next few days we saw M. Clemenceau ; M. Venizelos ; Senator White of U.S.A. ; M. Hymans, P.M. of Belgium ; Mr. Massey, P.M. of New Zealand ; Sir Robert Borden, P.M. of Canada ; Mr. G. N. Barnes and Lord Robert Cecil (now Lord Cecil of Chelwood), who as usual gave us every kind of help. We were also received at the Élysée by the President and his wife.

These interviews were extraordinarily interesting. We thought we detected in several of those who received us a curiosity to see what kind of wild-fowl the British and American Suffragists were. We had resolved not to speak to them about Women's Suffrage, feeling that each country might very well consider this a domestic not an international problem, but without exception as soon as we appeared they talked to us at once about it. M. Clemenceau—the "Tiger" as he was called—began at once, "There is not a single argument in favour of giving the vote to men which is not equally applicable to women. But——" And then followed a long disquisition on the dangerous power of the clergy over the minds of women. We suggested that possibly they had gained this power because they had, in spiritual things, admitted the equality of the sexes; but he did not give any encouragement to this line of argument. A few days later his life was attempted by a half-crazy youth who nearly succeeded in murdering him, and we thought that possibly this might have suggested that the other sex was specially amenable to an influence even less desirable than that of the clergy.

We were very much impressed by his vitality and energy and power of amusing repartee. The Tiger did not growl, he purred. His parting word to us was this: "*One word of advice: the moment you are unanimous, dissolve, separate.*

President Wilson, just before he left Paris on his return to the United States, wrote to me as follows:

PARIS,
14th February 1919.

My dear Mrs. Fawcett,

I did not fail to take up with my colleagues at the Quai d'Orsay your suggestion about a Commission of Women. I found practically all the conferees entirely sympathetic with the cause of Women Suffrage, but, if I may say so, embarrassed by the objections raised by representatives of India and Japan to a world-wide investigation, which would raise questions most inacceptable to them. It was evident that to press the matter would lead to some unpleasant controversies, and I concluded that I might be doing the cause more harm than good by insisting.

I am extremely sorry, and I hope and believe that the cause can be advanced in other ways.

In unavoidable haste,

Sincerely yours,
Woodrow Wilson.

In reference to the above it is not a little satisfactory to know that since 1919 women in Madras, Bombay, the United Provinces, and Burma have been enfranchised by the free vote of their own representative assemblies, as well as the women in the native States of Cochin, Travancore, and Jahalwar ; thus showing how misplaced were the fears respecting India expressed to President Wilson by his colleagues in Paris.

I must now close this recital of my remembrances and say good-bye to my readers. I have had a happy fifty years out of my seventy-seven in working for the advancement of women's freedom, and a happy few months in writing down what I remember. I should have wished to dwell on what I remember of two most interesting visits to Palestine in 1921 and 1922, but these memories are being reserved for another place. I hope it is not presumptuous in making my farewells to say that I do so with "a cheerful confidence in things to come."

INDEX

Printed in Great Britain by
UNWIN BROTHERS, LIMITED, LONDON AND WOKING

CPSIA information can be obtained
at www.ICGtesting.com
Printed in the USA
BVHW04s1036210618
519641BV00016B/341/P

9 781334 953422